SINGLE, SAVED & CELIBATE

A Real Woman's Guide To Getting It All Without Giving It Up

DR. DENISE LUTCHER

Bloomington, IN  Milton Keynes, UK

authorHOUSE®

AuthorHouse™
1663 Liberty Drive, Suite 200
Bloomington, IN 47403
www.authorhouse.com
Phone: 1-800-839-8640

AuthorHouse™ UK Ltd.
500 Avebury Boulevard
Central Milton Keynes, MK9 2BE
www.authorhouse.co.uk
Phone: 08001974150

First published by AuthorHouse 1/15/2007

ISBN: 978-1-4259-8977-4 (sc)

Library of Congress Control Number: 2006911317

Printed in the United States of America
Bloomington, Indiana

This book is printed on acid-free paper.

ACKNOWLEDGEMENTS

I would first like to thank God, for all He has done in and through my life.

Thanks to my sister Bernie, who always stands in my corner cheering the loudest.

Thanks to my Pastor, Dr. Tony Williams, who never gave up on me.

Thanks to Ms. Janice who listened as each chapter unfolded and wouldn't let me quit until the work was finished.

And thank you very much to the women who have attended my workshops over the years. Our God has great things in store for you.

Contents

INTRODUCTION

If you are a woman who has always made the right decisions; if you are a virgin determined to wait for that one special man God is preparing to be your lifelong mate; if you have never struggled through unhealthy relationship choices; if you've never cried yourself to sleep over the wrong man, this probably isn't the book for you.

On the other hand, if you are divorced, widowed, or coming to know the Lord after your thirtieth birthday; if you have a couple of kids; if you carry your share of wounds from love's many battles; or if you are simply struggling with the question of how anyone with normal thoughts or urges manages to remain celibate (and content), you will want to keep reading. The lessons I'm about to share were learned the hard way. I'm one *Real Woman* who didn't always make the right choices. I've struggled with the challenge of remaining celibate most of my adult life. It's a battle I sometimes won and sometimes lost. But at the end of the day, at this point in my journey, I simply refuse to allow the enemy to have the final word. Instead, I've chosen to use what I've learned to expose his lies and help other *Real Women* in their struggle to live *Single, Saved & Celibate.*

I cannot count the number of times I have wondered why there is no *Real Woman's* guide on the subject of celibacy. I've also lost count of the number of times friends, colleagues, and clients have said, "You really ought to write a book about this." It seems simple enough on the surface. God's Word says it's wrong to have sexual relations outside of marriage. I understand that to mean that if I am not married to a man, God doesn't want me to have sex with him. "But what does that *really* mean?" That's the question most people ask me. After all, one woman's "sex" might be another woman's "foreplay," right? And does the boundary of "no nothing" (oral, anal, or vaginal) only really apply to virgins?

Okay, so here's where the group who wanted to keep reading just a few paragraphs ago may be getting skeptical. Well, if you were looking for clever euphemisms about sex, you might want to brace yourself. I don't pull any punches from the beginning to the end of this work. This is *A Real Woman's Guide,* and we are talking about sex, so we will be talking about sex *for real.*

Likewise, if you were hoping for some type of sexual loophole (perhaps a description of all the ways to nearly give it up while still remaining within the lines), sorry to disappoint, but this isn't that kind of book either.

But there is good news: For the *Real Woman* who honestly desires to live holy, but who is struggling to find a way to do so while maintaining her identity as a beautiful, vibrant, mature, fun, and yes, sensual woman, do I have a recipe for you! The ten lessons I'm about to share with you represent foundational principles for healthy loving. Think of them as essential platforms upon which you can build a healthy relationship, or even strengthen an existing one. So grab a cup of coffee or tea, sit back, settle into your favorite chair, and take a real look inside your heart. *Single, Saved & Celibate* is not just a theory. *Real Women* just like you and me are *Getting It All Without Giving It Up* every single day—you can too.

Lesson #1

Loneliness Is Not Fatal

The first thing I need you to understand is that loneliness will not kill you. It may sting like the dickens, and you might wish you could lay down and die (if only to cause the last or current bad dating choice to realize what he's lost), but when it's all said and done, you will survive this awful feeling. You will live, and yes, you will even love again. You have the ability within you to survive, even if you don't recognize it, even if your life circumstances have caused you to doubt it. Just hold on. Help is on the way.

The feeling of loneliness is a lot like the sound of darkness. It's cold and a little hollow, so it reverberates against the walls of your heart and your mind. The sound gets louder and the feeling deeper, until it threatens to either deafen you or simply swallow you up whole. I know the feeling, because emotionally, I've been where you're living. A heart mending can feel an awful lot like a heart breaking. It's the weight of the memories, I suppose. We all miss the kind of love that's obvious and breathtaking during those awful, lonely times. We miss having someone in our life who really desires to be with us and who will protect and cherish us.

The hurt is there and it's real. And if you want to get past it and heal, you must come to understand this one simple truth, deep within your soul: This feeling, this horrible, lonely feeling that seems to reach further inside you than anything you've ever felt before, will in fact pass.

Loneliness in this context is similar to a muscle strain. It is the result of some type of injury or unanticipated trauma. Under normal conditions (like when you are busy working or caring for children), loneliness feels like a dull ache. It's there, just under the surface, to remind you that you've been hurt, but it's not really debilitating. Then, one day, the weather conditions change (like when you're all by yourself, when you hear a certain song, or when you get stood up for a date you didn't really feel like accepting in the first place) and wham! The sadness swells up and threatens to overtake you. Just like that, the pain goes from dull to intense to unbearable, in no time flat.

This is the point in time when most of us head for the cookie jar or the liquor cabinet or the wrong man's arms. We are desperately looking for a way to bridge the dark space between our hurt and our healing. The sad thing, ladies, is that as Malcolm X said, "...we have been tricked, hoodwinked, bamboozled." And thousands of years before Malcolm, Scripture said it even more clearly:

> *Do not gloat over me my enemy! Think I have fallen. I will*
> *rise. Though I sit in darkness, the Lord will be my light*
> *Micah 7:8.*

In short, the distance between our hurt and our healing is not nearly as far as the enemy of our soul would have us believe. Why would the enemy care whether or not you believe things will ever get better? Because if he can get you to believe the lie that loneliness is fatal, he can get you to compromise your principles, your health, your happiness, and ultimately your intimacy with the Lord in an attempt to "feel better."

All too often, I see intelligent, beautiful, gifted sisters falling for the lie. We give in and give it up, only to realize a temporary solution won't fix anything at all, because the solution is not real.

The good news is that loneliness no longer need be your bottomless pit. There is a way up and out of the lonely trap. You have options. From this day forward, you can reframe the way you view loneliness. You can choose to do something positive to get through the feelings, rather than allowing them to control you. Ask yourself if you are ready to learn the lesson: Loneliness is not fatal.

Remember, we who are in Christ are never really alone. Nothing can separate you from Him.

> *For I am convinced that neither death nor life, neither angels nor demons, neither the present nor the future nor any powers, neither height nor depth, nor anything else in all creation, will be able to separate us from the love of God that is in Christ Jesus our Lord.*
> *Romans 8:38-39 NIV*

If you are not quite convinced, reread this chapter and commit to pray about the message before moving forward. I believe God is preparing and strengthening an army of strong women to move forward in life and in ministry. It is not by chance that you have chosen this study. If you are feeling uncertain, give it time. God is faithful; He promises never to leave or forsake you *(Deuteronomy 31:6.)* He promises to give you what you need to make it. *(Matthew 7-8.)* God wants to heal your hurt and restore your joy. He desires to prosper and not harm you *(Jeremiah 29:11)*. Let's move to higher ground together.

LESSON #2

In for a Penny, in for a Pound

In for a penny, in for a pound; in for a dime, in for a dollar; give an inch, take a mile. They all mean the same thing. Without healthy limits and boundaries, what seems like a little harmless flirting, fun, or game-playing (the penny) can all too quickly lead to you giving it up (the pound). Dancing too close to the flame is a mistake too many *Real Women* continue to make, often with devastating results. When it comes to the many aspects of a romantic relationship, healthy limits and boundaries are essential. We must guard our hearts *(Jeremiah 10:23)* and our steps *(Proverbs 4:23)* if we are to succeed in our quest to *Get It All* without having to compromise.

It is important for *Real Women* to realistically evaluate how much physical contact is safe and acceptable for them to have. Just because your best friend can handle a romantic evening listening to music and sipping fine wine in front of a warm fire doesn't mean that is a safe environment for you. We all have individual triggers or areas of vulnerability that we have to guard. I cannot emphasize enough how your threshold of physical, environmental, and emotional tolerance is particular to you. God created you as a unique individual. You have lived a unique life, with experiences and circumstances that shape your reaction to stimuli. I'm challenging you to think about the range of possibilities and honestly evaluate where your physical, environmental, and emotional boundaries should be set. Consider the following guidelines while mapping your course.

Physical Boundaries: This one isn't as difficult as it may seem. Our bodies and our spirits generally give us clues or indications that we are nearing the point of no return. The data is there; we just choose to ignore it. As *Real Women*, we need to start by first getting to know ourselves, which means we need to know our own bodies, our strengths, and our vulnerabilities. Next, we need to begin listening to our own inner voice when it tries to warn us to stop because there's a cliff up ahead.

Practically speaking, if holding hands and hugging is okay for you, but kissing makes you weak in the knees, set the stopping place before the kiss. If a "French" or open-mouthed kiss sends you to the wrong place, refuse to open your mouth, except of course to explain why you don't French kiss.

Pay attention to what your body and your spirit are telling you about you. If you are thinking, "I really need to go home," you probably do. If you are thinking, "I really shouldn't be doing this," you probably shouldn't. One wonderful thing about *Real Women* is that we have life experience. If pressed to do so, we can quite accurately describe the places, people, things, and behaviors that cause us the most harm, based upon our own history, based upon fact, rather than speculation.

Consider the following points about environmental and emotional boundaries:

Environmental Boundaries: It is best to decide up front, before you agree to that first date, whether or not you are comfortable with the man knowing where you live. This is especially important if you live alone. If you are uncertain, agree to meet in a neutral location, and arrange your own transportation to and from the designated site. Having your own transportation will allow you to increase your comfort level from a safe distance, and if things get dicey, you will have the ability to excuse yourself and get home hassle-free.

If you are past the first-date stage, consider whether or not you are comfortable visiting his home or apartment. This point may go beyond the issue of comfort and really be about personal safety. If you are not feeling safe (and your instincts will most likely let you know), you might want to reconsider dating this man at all. Despite propaganda being espoused by the media about the desperate shortage of men, there are other fish in the sea. God wants you to have the man He designed and prepared for you. Don't sell yourself short. Don't disregard God's plan for you by settling for less than what you deserve. Refer to Lesson # 4 if you are concerned about safety and are wondering if the man you are dating could potentially be abusive.

But I digress ... we were discussing <u>environmental boundaries</u>. Consider carefully what kind of social activities you are comfortable engaging in. In today's social climate, a typical "date" movie may be filled with intense bedroom scenes that start your imagination (and your libido) off and running. You might love to dance, but choosing an intimate jazz club or blues hangout for dancing, rather than listening purposes, may not be in your best interest. Don't misunderstand— there's nothing inherently wrong with going dancing on a date, but if you choose to spend the better part of the evening sipping alcohol and slow dancing in the arms of a man you are attracted to (and trust me, after that second glass of wine, attraction becomes relative) you may have to work harder than otherwise necessary to say good night at your doorstep.

Speaking of doorsteps, this brings us to the <u>environmental boundary</u> that is your front porch. For many *Real Women,* this is the moment of truth. You went out, had a great meal where you didn't have to cut anybody's meat or mop up spilled milk. Nobody called you Mama, unless it was in a good way. You body was adorned in silk or chiffon because you didn't have to worry about spit-up or sticky fingers. Somebody opened the door, walked on the sidewalk closer to the street, held your hand, paid for dinner, and left a good tip. To top it off, he made you laugh and feel like a woman. In short, you had a wonderful evening and you simply do not want it to end.

Time out! Better yet, time to use your tools. It's time to *Stop, Look,* and *Listen...*

STOP ... Resist the urge to turn your brain off. Now is not the time to click on the autopilot switch. Refusing to think at this moment may lead you to a place you will later regret going. Besides, if your date had half the great time you did (and you should be able to tell), he will be back.

LOOK ... Pay attention to your date's behaviors. Has he suddenly grown an extra pair of hands? Are you struggling to keep those hands off of the body parts that he doesn't have permission to touch? If the moment on your porch involves a kiss, is it warm and tender or voracious and overwhelming? If he is behaving like he could swallow you whole, beware. It is only going to get more intense once you let him indoors.

LISTEN ... Is he speaking words of admiration and affirmation or is he attempting to guilt you into allowing him to come inside? Is he talking about seeing you again or is he trying to close the deal tonight? Remember, you are not available for rent or lease. He is not entitled to test-drive the merchandise, you do not come with dinner, and last but certainly not least, you are definitely worth the wait.

Once you've taken the quick *Stop, Look,* and *Listen* inventory, if you have determined the gentleman's words and actions are appropriate, and you have checked the appropriateness of your own thoughts and behaviors, there's nothing wrong with inviting the man inside. Again, you want to keep both your integrity and your testimony intact, so you may want to keep the following helpful hints in mind.

Hint #1: Decide exactly how long he can stay before you step through the door. It's not necessary to tell your date how long you've decided he can stay in minutes, but *you* should know. Use all your tools, ladies. "The kids are sleeping." "It's late and I still have to take the sitter home." "I have an early day tomorrow." "This has been great, but I'm exhausted." Any of these statements can be preceded by, "You are welcome to come in, but only for a few minutes, because ..."

Hint #2: If he declines to come in, don't insist. Say you understand, thank him for the evening, smile, and say good night. If he gets angry, consider that a warning sign (see Lesson #4—*How to spot an abusive man before it's too late*).

Hint #3: If he accepts your invitation to come inside, be careful not to let the time get away from you. Even if you are really enjoying his company, it is important to stick to the time limit you set for yourself. The more attracted you are to a man, the more important it is for you to discipline yourself to mean what you say, and say what you mean.

Once you are comfortably past the first (or early) dating phase, and are seeing someone regularly, you may need to determine where the danger zones are in your home, as well as where they are in your date's home. Again, this will be a very individual assessment; but for most *Real Women*, there's not really a good (enough) reason to entertain (or be entertained) in the bedroom. Still, for a select few, their bedroom may be the only space that belongs to them. If that is your situation, I recommend you keep the door open, and if possible, use chairs or some seating choice other than the bed.

I have one note of caution to share. While communication is always a good thing, edicts, on the other hand, are typically a bad thing. We *Real Women* can have a tendency to say too much, too soon. At times, we use our words like a force field. We eagerly rattle off a laundry list of what we will and will not do with a man (in vivid detail) over coffee. The problem is that most men take this as a challenge, and when they get us behind closed doors, it doesn't take much to discover we are willing to cross most, if not all, of the lines we've so eloquently described as unyielding and non-negotiable.

Might I suggest another tactic? Say exactly what you mean. Say it softly and in a normal speaking voice, with a smile, while looking him in the eye. Be firm and resolute, but never menacing. Answer the question being asked, and resist the urge to elaborate. When asked, or when dating someone more than once or twice, it is okay to tell him you are practicing celibacy. If asked for how long (and you will be), resist the urge to supply detailed information. A brief time may make it seem like you are not serious. A significant amount of time may make it seem like you are ready to give in. You might want to try simply responding with the phrase, "Long enough to be good at it," or "Long enough to know it is a good choice for me."

Please remember the decision to remain *Single, Saved & Celibate* is a personal choice. How we handle our sexuality is something each of us must decide for herself. Refrain from attempting to lecture your date (or anyone else, for that matter) into the fold. Your decision to live *Single, Saved & Celibate* is about you, not about the other person.

Emotional Boundaries: The concept of setting safe emotional boundaries can be a bit complicated, because some emotional cues are subtle and therefore difficult to detect. The key is to keep your eyes and ears open and to know what major potholes to avoid.

Pothole #1: Being emotionally dependent on your partner for validation or self-worth is not part of God's design for you *(I John 3:1-3)*. If you only think you look good when a man says so, that's a problem. If you allow your mood (good, bad, or indifferent) to be determined or shaped by your partner's mood, you are giving away too much power. If your partner is the only one who can make you believe things are going to be all right, you may be worshipping at the wrong altar. Think of your feelings as a kind of barometer of your emotional health. If you spend the majority of your life on the edge, one romantic crisis after another, honeymoon one minute and divorce court the next, this may be due in part to unhealthy emotional boundaries.

Pothole #2: Being in love is not emotionally equivalent to being foolish. God gave you a mind and the ability to use wisdom in making decisions *(Ephesians 5:15-17)*. Don't waste the gift. If a man is asking you to prove your love by remaining in a relationship that is overly controlling or overly critical, rather than edifying, that's a problem. Ask yourself how you feel during and immediately after spending time with him. Resist the urge to minimize or excuse inappropriate behavior. Call it what it is: an unhealthy emotional boundary, and purpose yourself to deal with it. Communicate how you feel when he speaks or behaves in a way that crosses your emotional boundaries. Discuss how you would prefer to be spoken to, and require that he respect you if he desires to remain in your life.

Pothole #3: Often people, who have a difficult time setting emotional boundaries (Pothole #2,) have an equally difficult time respecting other people's boundaries. If a man has not expressed a commitment to date you exclusively, you have no right to go off the deep end and accuse him of cheating or being unfaithful when you learn he is seeing someone else. If he is not your boyfriend (clue: he does not introduce you as his girlfriend); your fiancé (clue: you are not wearing a ring and there has not been a public announcement of your engagement); or your husband (clue: there was not an actual wedding ceremony) you are in no position to make emotional demands.

Requiring that he phone you daily to prove his love and intentions is simply unrealistic. Interpreting the absence of a daily call to be rejection is foolish. In the same vein, attempting to guilt, force, or manipulate another individual into sharing more about himself, his life, or his emotions than he wants to can be an example of blurred emotional boundaries. His stuff is his stuff. You do not have the right to insist he opens up the pages of his life and discloses all his deepest thoughts and feelings, just because you have. Respect is an essential part if any healthy relationship. If you want people to trust you with their story and their pain, it is important to create an emotional environment that's healthy enough for that to happen safely. Be available, be reassuring, be patient. And when others choose to share with you, treat the information as you would precious cargo. Emotional boundaries can be fragile by their very nature. Once someone adjusts his boundaries, allowing you to move in closer, be careful not to blow it by becoming: a) too verbal, b) too judgmental, c) too uninterested, or d) too eager to fix it. Just sit with the information. Then thank him for sharing his feelings with you and ponder what God would have you to do with the information.

Do not be anxious about anything, but in everything, by prayer and petition, with thanksgiving, present your requests to God. And the peace of God, which transcends all understanding, will guard your hearts and minds in Christ Jesus.
Philippians 4:6

Lesson #3

Somebody Is Confused—Is It You?

You may really be into your guy and into your relationship. You may be thoughtful and considerate, willing to share your time and energy with this man, because you love him. You may take extra care to fix yourself up and put your very best foot forward when you are together. You may work hard to listen and communicate. You may be willing to compromise in order to build a good relationship. You may willingly sacrifice to support his dreams, and work hard to understand when he is in a rotten mood. In short, you are fully committed, and you desire a future with this man.

If this describes you, like it or not, it's time to admit that you are definitely feeling this guy. The question remaining is … is this guy feeling you? You know you are his woman; but does he consider himself to be your man?

Even *Real Women* can sometimes be so determined to make a relationship work that we fail to see what is right in front of our face. When a man loves a woman (as the songwriter said) there's nothing he won't do. No obstacle is too great, no price is too high, no timeframe is too short, *to keep him from getting to you.* If there is something or someone preventing the two of you from being together, he will overcome it. If he only has a few minutes (or days) to spend in your neck of the woods, he will ask to spend them with you. If you phone, he will take the call, even if only to say he can't talk. If he misses your call, he will phone back, even if you didn't ask him to. If you are hurt, scared, or in need, he will come to your rescue. If you are indeed the one he is feeling, he will cherish and protect you (almost instinctively), the way God designed it to be. You will be high enough on his priority list that your care and safety will be extremely important to him.

Allow me to share one brief word of caution. If you are a woman who has made a habit of abusing your man's care and concern, you may have simply worn him out emotionally. In my experience, this does not typically happen when a woman is really feeling her man, but rather when she is using him (and sometimes others) to meet her needs outside of a committed relationship. For the most part, women who are desirous of a healthy, committed relationship are less likely to play emotional games with their man, just to see if he will come running.

This chapter is not intended to describe the manipulative type of relationship; However if find yourself repeatedly practicing manipulative patterns of behavior, you may find it beneficial to refer to lessons 8 and 10.

One way to determine whether or not you and the man you are dating have the same level of interest in, and commitment to, one another is to Stop, Look, and Listen. (Yes, that again!)

STOP … Stop making excuses for why he has not called or did not respond, and ask him. It is important this be done in an open, non-judgmental way. It is not a good idea to have this conversation when either of you is angry. When attempting to open up a dialogue, it is a good idea to stay away from "why" questions. Why questions tend to elicit defensiveness, which can lead to a very unproductive conversation.

Instead of asking why, try asking "What happened?" or asking "Did I understand you correctly when you said you were going to ...?"

Remember, women and men tend to communicate differently. The same words can have different meanings. When you say, "I'll be right there," you may mean you plan to go from point A to point B in the least amount of time possible. When a man says, "I'll be right there," he may very well mean he will leave point A, en route to destination point B, as soon as the game is over, and after he stops for gas, thereby arriving at point B in the least amount of time possible, considering the things he had to do first.

Obtaining correct and accurate information is important. Doing so can prevent or minimize misunderstandings between you and your man. And while few would argue with the need to gather accurate information, the methods of data collection vary widely. I would suggest you choose a respectful, non-threatening means of obtaining the information you want. You are not running a detective agency, nor are you questioning a key witness in a major trial; so now may not be the proper time to press your man for answers. Simply speak to him the way you would want to be spoken to. Most grown men do not like being bullied or mothered (except by their mother.) I suggest you try using the approach of telling your man why you need or want the information you are seeking. For example, when he says, "I'll be right there," try responding with, "Can you give me an idea of how long it will be, so I can know if I have time to ... (cook, finish my work, run a short errand, etc.)." This kind of information-gathering approach, executed with the right tone and genuine effect, will most likely yield the information you need, without provoking an argument.

STOP ... Stop telling your family and friends your man has said or done things that he has not said or done. In an effort to convince others (and sometimes ourselves) that both the man and the relationship are the best thing ever, we can fall into the very unhealthy pattern of embellishing his words and deeds. I have known women to buy themselves gifts (jewelry, flowers, even cars) then turn around and tell family and friends that these gifts are from their man. I have known others to repeat or replay conversations where they claim their man has said the perfect phrase or supplied the perfect answer to a deep, emotionally stirring question. Romantic fantasies and intimate moments the likes of which Hallmark and Lifetime have never known are whispered to girlfriends over coffee or lunch. Sadly, a lot of what is repeated unfortunately is simply not true. If you find yourself making up stories about things your man has done or said that are not exactly accurate, this may be an indication that someone is confused. Is it you?

LOOK ... Take a cold, hard look at how both you and the man in your life prioritize your life and your time. Compare notes on where the relationship is on your priority list, versus where it is on his. For example, I once dated a man whose life-commitment priority list looked like this:

1. God
2. His adult daughter and her children
3. His career
4. His education
5. Any blood relative (brother, sister, etc) in crisis
6. A committed romantic relationship

By comparison, my priority list listed like this:

1. God
2. My children
3. A committed romantic relationship
4. My ministry
5. My extended family

So, being the intelligent, gifted, mature person I am, I agreed to be priority number six in his life, while keeping him as my priority number three. Can you guess how well that worked out? It was a big mistake. In the end, I simply could not pull it off emotionally. Every time he cancelled plans with me to rescue another emotionally stranded sibling, I got ticked. Every time he left the theater to answer a text message or call regarding his daughter's latest financial crisis, I got ticked. And finally, when he could never figure out a way to take time off to spend a summer day playing hooky with me, I got just plain angry and gave up.

LOOK ... I implore you, based upon firsthand experience, to look at your life priority list honestly. Looking at the naked truth, while uncomfortable, may help shake you out of denial about where you really stand. If you and the man in your life cannot agree to function at the same priority level as one another, then one of you is likely a little more (or less) into this relationship than the other. If not balanced, that inequity over time can lead to serious problems.

LISTEN ... If you are serious about determining whether the way you feel about this man is mutual, it is important that you really listen to what he is saying.

If you find yourself thinking, *what he meant was* ...instead of *what he said was* ...be careful. Generally speaking, men are less likely than women to speak in code. If he says he got busy and didn't think about calling you, that is most likely what he means. If he says he is going to his sister's birthday party and he doesn't invite you, he most likely prefers to go without you. If he says he needs some time and space, he means he wants to be left alone to sort things out.

LISTEN ... If he says he is not ready to settle down or commit, take him at his word. He means he is not ready to commit—not even to you. If you are ready to commit, and worse yet, you already consider yourself to be in a committed relationship with this man, you are living your side of the relationship equation as though you are spoken for. Somebody is confused, and that somebody is you.

LESSON #4

How to Spot an Abusive Man Before It's Too Late

If pressed to describe which chapter of this book is most essential for any *Real Woman* desirous of developing healthy, lifelong relationships, I would have to say this is it. For too long, *Real Women* have tolerated or ignored abusive treatment in all its forms (emotional, sexual, spiritual, and physical) all in the name of love. We catch ourselves doing the same thing over and over, expecting a different result—the layperson's definition of insanity. We label it (low self-esteem, codependency, etc.) … We pray about it (Lord, please change him.) … We misconstrue scripture (I'm supposed to submit.) … We make excuses (he just had too much to drink.) … We minimize it (Girl, I'm not thinking about him.) … We even lie about it (I fell down the stairs.).

The scary thing is that the other women in our lives are rarely fooled. Our sister friends know in their heart of hearts that something is very wrong, because long before any physical bruises or bumps appear, the effects of verbal and emotional abuse are visible to anyone with the mind (and heart) to notice.

In all of my work over the past twenty-five years, with abused women representing a full spectrum of ethnic, socioeconomic, and age ranges, one interesting commonality has emerged. Looking back, all those women could describe the warning signs which lead up to the actual act of physical abuse. Most *Real Women* have similar reactions when asked if they would have drawn a boundary or ended the relationship, had they known early on it was likely to eventually become physically abusive. "Absolutely!" they insist. "In a minute," they declare. "H---yes!" they say with attitude. When asked what they would tell other women, the response is always the same. Those who have survived say they would tell their sisters to "pay attention and do something before it's too late."

The majority of abusive relationships follow a fairly predictable pattern. Absent organic or chemically induced psychosis, this type of dysfunctional human behavior is progressive. Abuse almost certainly begins with possessiveness and mistrust, and if permitted to follow its natural course unchecked, the behavior will someday end in physical abuse.

The good news is that *Real Women* have extraordinary instinct and intuition on our side. Once we decide to pay attention, it is fairly easy to spot the early warning signs of a potentially abusive man. And once we acknowledge the signs, we can choose to set a clear boundary, indicating what behaviors are unacceptable; and if that does not work, we can choose to save ourselves by walking away with our dignity and our body intact.

In all fairness, I must explain that there is one prerequisite for gaining the ability to fairly and objectively evaluate a relationship with a man you care for (or love), but are not married to … Ready? Here it is: *You cannot be sexually involved, because having sex with a man will cloud your view of reality.* It's not that you can't see what's going on when you are sleeping with a man. It's just that you see it through a different, rather foggy lens. The striations and murky nature of this distorted vantage point encourage you to create an alternate reality, an unhealthy world in which you are more willing to compromise and settle for what's being dished out, rather than insisting on or requiring what you deserve.

Every human being has the right to be treated with dignity and respect. How much more so, you a single woman under the protection and care of her father God, her husband, Jesus Christ, and her comforter, the Holy Spirit. You are, after all, *Woman,* the Crown of God's Creation *(Genesis 1:27, 31)*. And as such, respect is your birthright.

Consider the right to be cherished a birthright. Never allow anyone to convince you that you are not smart enough or thin enough or young enough to be treated with respect. Pay attention to how a man talks to and about you. Pay attention to how gentle or how rough his words and touch are. Pay attention to how short his emotional fuse is, what kinds of things set him off, and who is typically the target of that anger.

Over the next few pages, I will address a common spectrum of abusive behaviors. I encourage you to read through each category completely and prayerfully. I am not advocating that you see things in your relationship that are not there. We do not desire to promote or create paranoia. Rather, I am suggesting that *honesty* is crucial. Trust your instincts. Resist the urge to excuse, minimize, rationalize, or ignore what is real. Remember the admonition of your sisters: "Pay attention and do something, before it's too late."

Types of Abuse and Related Warning Signs

Emotional or Psychological Abuse
The hallmark of emotional or psychological abuse is the mental suffering inflicted upon the person being abused. Isolation, intimidation, and manipulation are favored weapons of the abuser. The emotionally

abusive partner may simply disappear whenever he doesn't get his way. He may refuse to answer his phone, alternating between letting the phone ring and turning it off altogether, just to mess with you. He may intentionally cause you to fear for his safety by driving recklessly following a heated discussion. After refusing to acknowledge whether he made it home safely, he may then behave as though you are making a mountain out of a molehill when you finally reach him at work two days later.

The intimidation tool can have an equally irritating and confusing effect on your psyche. Intimidation is being employed as an emotional abuse tool when your partner uses the fact that he is not physically abusive to keep you in line. He might swell up or get very intense. He might even throw things at or near you. The explosion can be sparked by almost anything that upsets him. And while it may not silence you, it may have the desired effect of reminding you who is bigger and stronger, and just one step away from losing it. The intimidator's behavior creates the illusion that he can't help himself. It looks as though you've pushed him too far and something had to give. Of course, the message that it's not his fault is exactly what the act of intimidation is meant to convey. Namely, that the abuser is the victim; that his behavior is outside of his control; that something or someone is "making" him behave this way.

Remember, as adults, we are each responsible for our own behavior *(Romans 14:12)*. No one can make us abuse another human being. The decision to do so is just that, a decision. Abusing another person is a choice. It is a deliberate act. Justifying abusive behavior does not excuse it or explain it away.

The manipulation weapon is a more subtle but nonetheless destructive method of emotional abuse. The manipulator engages in emotional blackmail to get you to do things his way, in his time, with his permission, or not at all. He may imply that he plans to take you out just long enough to get you to turn down an invitation to join your family, then show up late and tell you he's too tired to go out. When you make plans to hang out with your girls for a change, he may pout or allow you to overhear him making plans to hang out with a negative peer group or another woman. This behavior is designed to manipulate you into changing your plans. He desires to have your undivided attention, even when he refuses to give you his.

If you are insightful or strong enough to see through the manipulation and resist the urge to change your plans, the manipulator may respond by persistently calling or text messaging you while you are away—to check on you, to see that you are all right, to apologize for his behavior, to say he's thinking about you, to inquire when you are coming home, or to say he needs help with the kids.

Although these points of contact may be framed as care and concern, beware. If your partner is adept at manipulation, these messages are less about care and more about control. Remember, you are a grown-up, and as such, you are capable of getting from point A to point B unharmed. Chances are pretty good that you could survive a day or evening out unsupervised before you hooked up with your current partner. So ask yourself, is he checking on you for your welfare and peace of mind … or his? And do you have the same permission to check on him when he is out without you?

Spiritual Abuse

The nuances of spiritual abuse can be difficult to detect. For many *Real Women,* our early religious teachings influence our susceptibility to spiritual abuse. Despite where we are currently living our spiritual lives (in or outside of God's will), spiritual abuse can be difficult to detect. Most of us can recall early childhood memories of church attendance, Sunday school or catechism, and bedtime prayers. Even if we really didn't know God in a personal way (through Jesus) we certainly knew of Him.

The lack of a personal, intimate relationship with Christ may be a big part of what makes us so vulnerable to spiritual abuse. Knowing God from a distance makes us dependent upon other people's interpretation of His character. As children or young adults, we were too often frightened into obeying an angry God, whom we believed would punish us if we did not do exactly as told. Love and forgiveness were concepts our teachers glossed over, because they did not fit the instructors' agendas. Like Adam and Eve, we learned to try and hide the things we were ashamed of *(Genesis 3:8)*. We came to expect judgment when God wants to offer grace *(Hebrews 4:16)*.

With that kind of history as a backdrop, we typically wandered away from the church after coming of age. Out on our own, with a new sense of freedom, we experimented with new ideas, new lifestyles, and new choices. In retrospect, some decisions were good, some were bad, and a few were just plain crazy. We grew up, got tired of living life separated from God, and eventually found our way to (or back to) Christ.

Even *Real Women* have to face the truth that most of us came to the kingdom of believers with very little actual knowledge of the scriptures. Then, instead of learning to pray and grow in the Word once we found our way to church *(II Timothy 2:15)*, we warmed a pew once a week and expected a charismatic preacher to entertain and inform us.

You might be wondering what all this has to do with abusive relationships. The answer is "plenty." If you do not know what the Bible actually says about your place, your role, your value, and what your self-concept should be as a woman, it becomes too easy for a man to misinterpret the Word and use it to justify treating you in an un-Christlike manner.

Scripture says you are to submit yourself to your *husband (Ephesians 5:22-24)*, not to your Baby Daddy, who happens to be sexually involved with both you and his ex-girlfriend at the same time.

Scripture says your body is for the glory of God *(I Corinthians 7:34-35; Isaiah 43:1b)* and the mutual enjoyment of your *husband,* not your fiancé.

Scripture says your man is to leave his parents and prepare a house to bring his bride to *(Ephesians 5:31)*, not move into your room at your mama's house.

Scripture says finding a wife is a pleasure, not a burden *(Proverbs 18:22)*.

I am continuously amazed at how adept abusive men are at misusing scripture to convince intelligent, attractive, *Real Women* to put up with outrageous (and unhealthy) behavior. God does not want us to be fooled. We are to be wise as serpents and gentle as doves *(Matthew 10:16)*. Jesus came so that we could have life and have it more abundantly *(John 10:10)*. Wisdom, gentleness, and abundance of love should be hallmarks of your romantic relationships as well. Your man should be praying both with and for you. God's word should be uttered in ways that are uplifting and encouraging. Of course we know God's word is useful for correction and reproof *(II Timothy 3:16)*; but even words of correction should be spoken in love.

In sum, if your partner uses scripture to degrade, embarrass, hurt, condemn, or control you, he may be spiritually abusive.

Sexual Abuse

I purposely separate sexual abuse from physical abuse, because I believe it warrants special attention. Sexual abuse in the Christian community is one of those difficult subjects which we find easier to ignore than address. Like anything unholy which is hidden away in the shadows and whispered about, sexual abuse (if ignored) will continue to grow wild, untended, and out of control, until it simply takes over and destroys anything healthy around it. Once the healthy parts of your relationship have been contaminated and destroyed, all that will remain will be deformed, malnourished, anemic, and just plan sick. Left to its own devices, sexual abuse, like any other form of abuse, will eventually destroy any relationship.

Forms of sexual abuse can range from very subtle (e.g. unwanted kissing or touching) to very direct (e.g. rape or sexual assault.) What makes it abuse? In layperson's terms: If you didn't want it to happen, and you told him you didn't want it to happen or you attempted to prevent or stop it from happening, and he did it anyway, that's abuse. Let's be clear—I am not after political correctness here. I am saying quite simply, if you made a decision concerning your body that your partner refused to respect, he is wrong. Is it fair for you to change your mind at the last minute? Maybe not, but that does not negate your right to do so. Nobody has the right to force you to touch or be touched against your will. Doing so is abusive.

Sexual abuse in the form of date rape is not just happening across our high school and college campuses, it is also taking place in our high-priced corporations and even in our churches. In the case of date rape, women know and typically are at least initially attracted to the abuser. They may spend weeks or months flirting and getting to know one another before actually dating. After agreeing to see one another socially (perhaps one, two, or even more times) things get more intense until one day (or night), the woman finds herself in a sexually compromised or dangerous situation. She says no, and he refuses to stop. Despite her decision not to have sex or physical contact, he forces her to do so. That is sexual abuse, and it is wrong.

A word of caution here: Please remember that wanting to have sex, agreeing to have sex, enjoying the physical act of sex, then later resenting your partner because it was, in fact, just sex (and not a relationship) he desired, may be a humiliating or hurtful experience, but it does not qualify as abuse. It is important (once again) that you be honest with yourself and with your partner. If you mean no, say no, and get out of there; even if you have to struggle, to do so. It is your body, which means it is up to you to take control. If you do not have a voice in this relationship, then it may not be a healthy relationship for you. Today is the day to do something about it. You may not get another chance.

Physical Abuse

The simple definition of physical abuse is when anyone physically injures you by any means other than accidental means (California Penal Code CPC 11165.6).

When most people think of abuse, they picture or imagine physical abuse. Made-for-TV movies and films have done much to bring the topic of physical abuse into the spotlight. Unfortunately, these depictions often stereotypically describe low-income or ethnic minority people or groups, fighting over money or drugs. The truth is that domestic violence happens in every stratum of society. Among young, old, rich, poor, majority, minority, urbanites and suburbanites alike; domestic violence is an equal-opportunity crime.

The physical abuse form of domestic violence includes pushing, pulling, hitting, shoving, grabbing, kicking, punching, choking, cutting, etc. The act does not have to leave a bruise or mark to qualify as abuse. The act does not have to require medical attention or involve broken bones or bleeding. You don't have to be married or living with the individual. Anytime anyone willfully inflicts physical injury or harm upon you, their behavior qualifies as physical abuse.

Even *Real Women* sometimes ask me if it is still abuse if they "made" their partner hit them. The simple answer is yes. Even if you believe something you said or did prompted or elicited a violent response, your actions do not change the fact that it is still abusive. If you hit him first, then you are both guilty of physical abuse. If you yelled or screamed or threw things first, then you are guilty of emotional abuse; and if he hit you, he is still guilty of physical abuse.

The complicated answer to whether or not it is still abuse if you "made" him do it is still yes. No one can make another individual do or not do anything. We all possess the gift of free will. Every man and woman is responsible for his or her own actions. *(Romans 14:12).* The decision to abuse another is a choice. If we make that choice, we alone are responsible. In the rare incidence of self-defense, an individual is defending or protecting him- or herself (a defensive posture) rather than attacking (an offensive posture). A defensive posture is typically connected with an attempt to flee or get away from danger. A person defending him- or herself is typically not the aggressor.

Irrespective of the form of abuse (emotional, spiritual, sexual, or physical) there is a behavioral pattern common to abusive relationships, known as the Cycle of Violence.

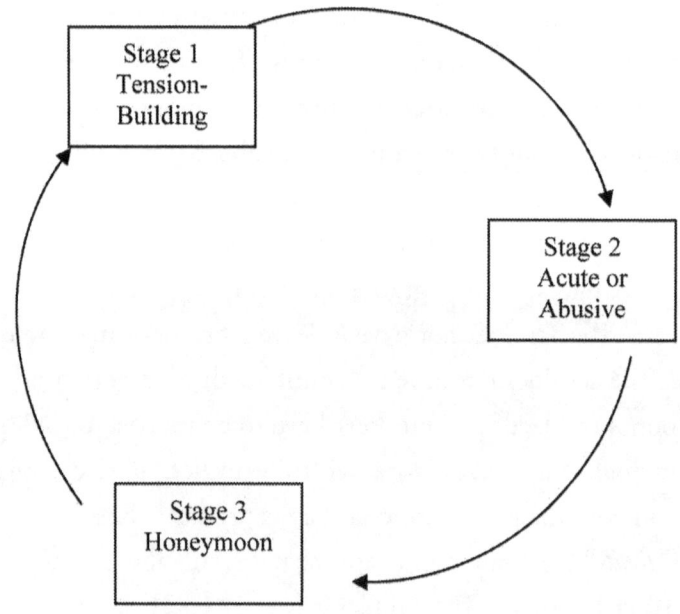

The Cycle of Violence involves the progressive stages of a repetitive cycle. Left uninterrupted, the cycle will continue to repeat itself until either one of the partners is removed or someone dies.

Stage 1

Stage 1 is known as the **tension-building stage** because it is characterized by an atmosphere of enhanced or heightened anxiety within the relationship. The person likely to be abused is being very careful to say and do the "right" things. She is "holding her breath," "walking on eggshells," and "waiting for the other shoe to drop." The frightening reality is that there is no rhyme or reason to the progression of violence. What might move this couple from Stage 1 to Stage 2 today might be totally different than what prompted the escalation in the past. For example, calling to say hello might be viewed as a deliberate invasion of privacy today, while failing to call might be interpreted as a deliberate effort to ignore or disrespect the abuser tomorrow.

Stage 2

Stage 2, the **acute phase**, is the most violent and therefore the most dangerous of the three stages. If the past abuse has been emotional or spiritual, this stage is where it will intensify. The intent at this stage is to inflict serious damage; not to simply shut you up, but rather to physically dominate, control, or harm you.

If the past abuse has been physical, it will likely become more focused, severe, concentrated, and again intentional at this phase. Many describe this stage as the explosion or blow-up of tension or pressure described in Stage 1.

Stage 3

If a woman survives Stage 2, the relationship will enter Stage 3. This stage is commonly known at the **honeymoon stage,** because the abuser will typically express remorse, along with promising never to repeat the abusive behavior. He may also use this time to blame you for the abuse, by reminding you that he wouldn't get so angry if you would just start (or stop) doing something. He may bring gifts, beg for forgiveness, tell you he cannot live without you, even cry or plead for forgiveness. He desperately wants to make up, and things between you may seem as wonderful and romantic as when you first met. You may experience a range of emotions, from fear to anger to sadness to love. You may be embarrassed and confused. You may want to hold him, nurture him, and relieve his pain, all the while sorting through feelings of anger and disbelief regarding how things got so messed up in the first place. Eventually, if the pattern is uninterrupted, you will forgive him, and the cycle will repeat itself. The honeymoon stage will end and the tension-building stage will begin again.

If you find yourself trapped in an emotionally, spiritually, sexually, or physically abusive relationship, silence and complacency are not the answer. Nearly thirty years of experience working with people who are hurting has taught me one absolute in regards to abusive relationships: *They do not get better by themselves.* Left unchecked, uncorrected, unaddressed, underground, and undercover, abusive relationships get worse, until someone goes to jail, someone leaves, or someone dies.

If you are thinking things are not "that bad," or that it was "just that one time," please take a moment to review this chapter again. It could save your life.

LESSON #5

Dating 101—It's Just a Date!

It is my solemn belief that *Real Women* can prevent most dating disasters (or at least minimize the emotional fallout) my slowing down and adopting a healthy mindset about dating.

Like many words commonly used in our culture, the word "dating" has evolved to include any number of meanings. We use the word to describe someone we have just met and are interested in getting to know better. We use it to describe a relationship that is ongoing but not exclusive. We use it to describe a relationship that is exclusive but has not led to engagement. We use it to describe a relationship that involves sex but not marriage (the same way we use the word "friend"). It makes no sense at all. At the end of the day, we are not even sure what *we* mean when we say we are "dating" someone. And if we are not sure what it means to date someone, how in the world can we clearly communicate our expectations to another person?

Further, how is it possible to evaluate whether we are dating in a healthy or unhealthy way, when we don't even know what dating is?

What most women, even *Real Women,* term "dating" can best be described as "courting." We meet a man who we are attracted to (typically at a physical level) and we begin to imagine or wonder (almost instantly) if he is "the one." Before the end of the first official outing, we are looking, wondering, imagining, what it would be like to be his wife. We tell ourselves we are going to take it slow, but by date number three, we are already picking out the wedding dress and are hinting about how many carats the right size engagement ring would be.

Real Women are especially adept at falling in love. In fact, many of us are simply in love with the idea of being in love. The leading man may change, but the fantasy remains intact. Because the shadowy image of Prince Charming is really more of a caricature than a real person, we can get caught in that dreaded loop I like to call *serial monogamy*. We move from one relationship to the next, each one a basic carbon copy of the preceding one. From one man to the next, we never quite learn the lessons we need to learn to get it right.

Dating the wrong way is a big part of this dysfunctional cycle. If you want to get off the merry-go-round, stop courting and start dating. Let's begin with a clarification of terms.

Dating is for fun, social companionship, deepening friendship, and for screening potential boyfriends.

Courting, on the other hand, is marked by a deep level of emotional and spiritual intimacy. There exists a mutual agreement and desire for exclusivity. Neither party can imagine being with anyone else. Both are committed and growing as individuals and as a couple. You now have a boyfriend.

Engagement is when both parties have agreed and are currently working on preparing themselves physically, emotionally, spiritually, and financially to be married to each other for the rest of their lives. Engagement is a private decision which leads to a public announcement. You now have a fiancé.

When a *Real Woman* dates that right way, she takes care to remind herself that it is just a date. Dating is the process by which we discover what we like and do not like in the opposite sex. We are able to discover what we need to change about ourselves to be a good friend and companion. And most importantly, we can objectively determine what we are willing to give and take to be in a relationship. Dating is not an exclusive endeavor. Dating one person and one person only is likely to result in a lopsided arrangement in which a man is "dating" you, while you are "courting" him.

Any man who is not ready to court you cannot be forced or guilted into doing so by your decision to court him. What typically happens is he will simply continue to date others (in addition to you) in secret or private. When you find out and confront him, he will remind you that the two of you never agreed to date exclusively. He may say the other women are "just friends," and finally, if things get heated enough, he will admit that he is not ready to commit, often adding that if he were, it would certainly be to someone exactly like you.

You will feel hurt and betrayed, but the truth is you brought this heartache upon yourself. While there may be some truth to your claim that exclusivity was implied, monogamy is rightly attached to courting, engagement, and marriage, not to dating. Remember, dating is for fun, social companionship, self-improvement, and screening.

Managing early dating expectations can help you avoid falling into the dating disaster trap. When you meet someone, you need to pay attention to more than just the physical or sexual chemistry. The practical reason is because if that is all you have in common, it will be tough to think of anything the two of you can mutually enjoy except sex. And once sex becomes part of the relationship, it becomes almost impossible for most *Real Women* to just date a man. In your heart of hearts, he's now your man (even if he doesn't yet realize it) and your expectations of how he should feel and treat you shift accordingly.

Maintaining a proper balance and perspective when dating can best be achieved when you are dating more than one person. Clearly, you did not just "hear" me say "sleeping with more than one person." In fact, if you review the previous paragraph, you will recall that sleeping with anyone you are dating will almost certainly lead you away from the goal of *Getting It All.* So please understand, dating multiple people is not license or permission to have multiple sex partners.

That being said, where does a *Real Woman* find a good single man, much less two or more, and how in the world does she juggle them when she does? Well, there are actually plenty of eligible single men out there looking for good women. Some are divorced, some widowed, and a few have never been married. Most have one thing in common: They are looking for a date. They are not looking for a wife. That is how men are wired. They are not sitting around wishing they had someone to spend the rest of their lives with. Rather, they are thinking how great it would be to have a woman whose companionship they enjoy, to hang out with today. And the reality is that women are more fun to be with when we are simply enjoying the moment (i.e. dating). Sadly, most of us are far too preoccupied with what we think should come next (courting) to enjoy the dating moment. We are so busy trying to convince the man to want us that we don't take the time to honestly evaluate whether we really want him.

Face it, ladies, most men are commitment-phobic. They cringe at the thought of being hemmed in, afraid of losing their freedom and their independence. At the same time, they know God created them to be incomplete without us. So, deep down, men know they need and want a help mate. They just don't like having their hand forced. That is why when you are dating someone who *knows* you are God's woman for him, you don't have to force him to commit. He will ask you to stop seeing other men and move to the committed relationship (courting) stage with him. Why? Simply put, the fear of being without you is greater than the fear of giving up his independence.

One very important aspect of the progression from dating to courtship is that he as the man must lead, and you as the woman must follow. From dating to courting to engagement, through marriage, if you have to push, prod, threaten, or entrap a man, there's trouble up ahead. If the leadership roles are reversed, you will always wonder if you made him commit, and so will he. Trust me, it will come up later, and it will not be a pleasant discussion.

So how long does the full progression take? Well, that depends. If you are feeling him and he is feeling you, about six to nine months of real dating should lead you to the courting phase, meaning he is asking you to see him exclusively. If you agree, you are now courting (see earlier definition). This does not mean you have agreed to marry. You are not engaged. If you require an engagement to stop seeing other people, trust me, you are not ready to marry this man.

In the courting phase, you will first spend time determining whether you are ready to marry anyone, and if so, whether this man is the one. It takes time for you to know yourself and another person well enough to determine whether the relationship is right. If you are serious about this, the courting period should involve individual counseling or mentoring. This is not premarital counseling. This is not pre-engagement counseling. Some *Real Women* use counseling at this phase to meet requirements set down by their church or pastor. They have already set a wedding date, booked the location, and bought a dress. Couples mistakenly enter counseling to simply check off another box on their to-do list before the ceremony.

I have found the best way to undergo relationship counseling is to do so without public announcement or fanfare. The two of you do not need the pressure of others believing you are on a track you've not yet decided to be on. The only people who really need to know you are exploring taking the relationship to the next level (engagement) are the two of you and your counselor, pastor, or spiritual mentor. Discuss your mutual desire to explore taking this step, and begin to spend time with and around mature believers who know you, can speak into your lives, and who have healthy relationships with the opposite sex.

Next, begin to work independently with a counselor or mentor whom you trust to give honest feedback about you, and who will challenge you to grow as a Christian and as a person, separate and apart from each other.

Finally, agree on a timeline by which the two of your will evaluate your relationship and check in regarding your honest evaluation of whether you are ready to move to the next level, engagement.

Some of you may be thinking, this is all fine and well for new relationships, but you have been in a relationship for four, five, maybe even ten years or more. At this point, *Real Women* zealously point out to me that they are in love. They tell me they are in an exclusive relationship and they are happy. They believe that one day, "when he's ready," they will get married.

Okay, here it comes … you are not going to like it … are you ready? WAKE UP! If you are in this situation, you have likely moved yourself into the practical or emotional space of "wife" to this man without the benefit of marriage. It's like your grandmother always said, "Why buy the cow when the milk is free?" Even if you are not physically intimate, if you are cooking, cleaning, driving, parenting, and otherwise nesting with this man as though he were your husband, why would he want anything to change? He currently has the best of both worlds. You are committed, and clearly not going anywhere, and he has that reassurance (and thus the benefits) without the responsibility.

If you are the one who is against moving forward to engagement or marriage, then you are holding this man back. If his genuine desire is to be married, and he feels that is God's plan for his life, you are in the way. And being in the way of God's will is never a good place to be.

If you cannot imagine your life without this man, try imagining yourself five, ten, or fifteen years from now, stuck in exactly the same place. Only by then, you will have invested a decade or more of your life pouring yourself into something that has taken more out of you than you planned to give; leaving you with very little to show in return. If you think it will hurt to call the question now, what do you imagine it will feel like then?

Don't misunderstand. I am not suggesting that you put your man on a one-year plan to buy that ring and get down on one knee. I am suggesting, however, that you think this thing through. The clock really should not begin running until you are courting. There's not any real time limit on how long you can date someone, as long as you are doing it in a healthy way. Since you are not relying on any one dating partner as your only option, and you are not committed, when you get tired of them or if you decide you don't have much in common, the relationship will die a natural (and relatively painless) death. One or the other of you will simply stop calling. No scene, no drama, just fade to black.

On the other hand, if this is the man for you, you will likely find yourself happy to give up your other dating relationships to enter into an exclusive courtship when the time is right. From there, one to one and a half years in a courtship will either lead to an engagement, which will then likely led to an actual marriage within another one to two years, if it's done right; or there will be a mutual agreement to move on.

In short, healthy behavior on the front end (while dating) will pay off once you move to the more mature stages of relationship development (courting and engagement). But what does a *Real Woman* do if she is stuck in the gray zone, having moved too quickly from dating to courtship, with no clue if she will ever get to engagement? The first step is to acknowledge the mistake you made. The second step is to honestly evaluate whether this man and this relationship (just as they both are) are what you want. Ignore the little voice in your head telling you how much time you have invested, or how much better off you are than your single friends. Be honest with yourself. Are you sure this is the man God wants you to spend the rest of your life with?

If the answer is "no" or "maybe," talk to him. Make certain neither of you is tired or angry (or hungry), and that you have some privacy. Have the talk face-to-face, rather than over the phone or via e-mail, and remind yourself to listen as well as speak.

Next, own your part of the process to date. Resist the urge to blame or judge him. If you moved things along too quickly, say so. If you agreed to date him exclusively, not because you thought it was time, but because you were afraid of losing him, say so. If you have not completed the work you need to do to make yourself whole after a loss or previous bad relationship, say so. If you care for him and still desire to see him, but not exclusively, say so. If you know in your heart of hearts that he is not the one, and you are with him because it's familiar and comfortable, or because you do not want to be alone, say so, apologize, and release him.

If the answer is yes, you are certain this is the man God has for you, because He has revealed it or confirmed it through whatever means He uses to speak to your heart and mind, talk to your man. Again, acknowledge your part in all this.

If you moved things along too fast and now you are tired of waiting for the next step, say so. If the relationship began as (or became) physical, and that is preventing things from progressing and maturing, say so and tell him what you want to do about it. It will be difficult, but if the two of you really care for one another and are truly committed to putting Christ first in your relationship, you can get things back on track. If you are scared to be without him, but more frightened of just being his "friend" for the next five to ten years, say so and get off the merry-go-round.

The common theme is that it is time to find your voice, speak up, and do something. But remember, you can only control your side of the equation. We are talking about real life here, involving two human beings, each with free will. Be certain about how you feel before you take a stand. Pray about your questions and your conclusions. Trust that God's perfect will for your life is to prosper and not harm you *(Jeremiah 29:11.)* Understand that God knows your pain *(1 Corinthians 10:13)* and your tears have not been ignored *(Proverbs 56:8)*. As with many other things in your past, if you turn the area of dating over to God and let Him direct your path, things will work out for your good *(Romans 8:28)*. It will be hard, and at times it will be lonely, but when you are walking in the blessing God has prepared for you, a new lifetime with the man you are certain God wants you to be with, you will be glad you allowed Him to take control *(Proverbs 14:2)*.

LESSON #6

Travel Advisory

Single women traveling alone with men they are romantically involved with is a common occurrence today. A romantic weekend away without the kids is something all *Real Women* look forward to. Some say we within the Christian community are too concerned about the topic. After all, the critics in support ask, "What can you do away from home that you can't do at home?" Meanwhile, critics on the opposite side contend that the mere "appearance of evil" is sufficient reason to condemn the practice.

The primary purpose of this lesson is not to debate one side of the argument or the other. This lesson is not intended to help you decide whether or not to travel overnight with a man. Rather, it is intended to help you keep yourself safe and sane in the event you choose to do so.

As with most things in life, preparation, communication, and accountability are essential keys to success. Pretending that you have mastered temptation to the extent that traveling alone with a man is "no big deal" is a mistake. Likewise, loudly proclaiming how "grown" you are and being offended by anyone daring to hold you accountable is an even bigger mistake.

Yes, your decision to travel with a man is, in fact, your business, and you alone are responsible for your part in that decision. That said, we all know how easy it is to get tangled up in this web. Let's be real. Vacation sex is hard to resist. The thrill is part of the reason why married couples covet this kind of time away from kids, jobs, responsibilities, and real life. Being swept up in the moment, taking a break from reality, and separating ourselves from the mundane stuff is what vacation is all about. In a surreal vacation environment, it is easy to blur the boundaries, and thus, even *Real Women* can be tempted to compromise.

Even if the getaway does not involve candlelit romance and soft music, it almost always involves relaxation and fun. Add the issue of sleeping accommodations, and some *Real Women* who are attempting to live *Saved and Celibate* decide it's just not worth it to travel alone with a man after all.

On the other hand, for those who purpose within themselves that they can travel with a man without compromising themselves, I say where there is a will, there is a way. But before you pack your swimsuit, your sunscreen, and your little black dress, please make sure the keys of preparation, communication, and accountability are in your overnight bag. Make up your mind that you simply will not leave home without them.

Preparation Key: Do not allow the excitement or anticipation of getting away from it all to lull you into a false sense of security. If you and your travel companion have not established clear boundaries in regard to your physical relationship prior to departure, there is trouble up ahead. Trust me, there will be missed expectations, and one of you will likely end up pressuring the other to "relax" and "just let things flow."

There is only one problem with this so-called "just let things flow," approach. All streams, rivers, and canals naturally flow straight to the bedroom. Guilt and conviction are swept aside, and repentance is scheduled to surface the following morning, right after wake-up sex and breakfast. To make matters worse, because neither of you wanted to be accused of intending to have sex, you won't bring condoms. After all, packing condoms would signal premeditation. So, on top of feeling defeated, you are also feeling scared or concerned about unwanted pregnancy and sexually transmitted diseases. This is the point at which the enemy turns up the heat, telling you that life without sex is "impossible," and encourages you to keep it all secret. After all, he whispers, "what would the saints think if they knew you had fallen?"

Sound familiar? If so, know that you are not alone. We have all fallen short of the glory of God *(Romans 3:23)*. Be encouraged. God has big plans for you *(Jeremiah 29:11)*. And those plans include your romantic relationship.

Prepare for time away by first making a decision, independent of your companion, regarding whether or not you really need to stay the night. Is it possible to take a day trip? Do you need to spend the night because of physical distance or physical limitations, or do you merely want to spend the night? Remember, there is no right or wrong answer, as long as you are being honest with yourself. Denial is a very dangerous thing. Once we start lying to ourselves, we feel the need to support or embellish our lies with actions. Avoid the trap, by being honest with yourself. If you do not need to stay overnight, but you want to anyway, admit it.

If you decide to stay overnight, *prepare* by securing safe accommodations. If possible, plan to travel with another couple or stay in the home of trusted friends. This can serve to minimize or eliminate the pressure to share a room with your companion. Sharing space or staying with a friend can be especially useful if the expense of two rooms is cost-prohibitive.

If you decide to travel and stay alone, *prepare* ahead by reserving two rooms. If he is financing the trip, insist that you pay for your own room. Take care to communicate this need correctly (see communication key); but if you can't get the issue of accommodations settled before you leave home, do yourself a favor and stay home.

Finally if you choose not to have sex, *prepare* to have other singles label you old-fashioned, over-spiritual, arrogant, self-righteous, or frigid. In fact, *prepare* to be talked about and misunderstood. It comes with the territory. The guilt and conviction others feel about the choices they are making is too easily projected onto you. Practice telling people you have the right to live your life according to whatever standards you choose. And that for now, the decision to live *Saved and Celibate* works for you.

Resist the urge to judge or lecture others. Respect their right to live life the way they choose, and require that they do the same for you. In the end, those same friends and associates will end up asking you how to do it differently. And you will be perfectly positioned to show them the way *(Matthew 5:10)*.

Communication Key: All the preparation in the world will only get you so far without communication. We sometimes make great plans, agreements, and bargains (with ourselves) about what we are going to avoid or stop doing. The biggest problem with this approach is that we then self-sabotage our great planning by failing to communicate our intentions to anyone else. We keep our plans and promises secret, mainly so we can secretly reserve the option to fail. I am challenging you to take the option to fail off the table. Find your voice, open your mouth, and tell your travel companion what you need in order to feel safe when traveling with him.

There are several issues to consider. Perhaps all of the temptations involved support an agreement to actually be less physical with one another when you travel than you are at home. Or maybe you will agree to abstain from drinking alcohol while away. Perhaps a one-piece bathing suit is a safer choice than a thong bikini, if you want to keep his sexual desire for you within safe boundaries. Most certainly, good *communication* should include a discussion about sleeping accommodations.

Sharing a bed with a man you are attracted to without having sex is not evidence of your maturity or your willpower; it is merely foreplay. Sharing a room with a man you are attracted to without sleeping in the same bed is not a reasonable accommodation; it is foreplay at a distance, kind of like phone sex. Maybe not the first time; maybe not even the next time. But trust me, if you and this man continue to share sleeping accommodations, eventually you will end up in the same bed, at the same time, doing the same thing, and it won't be talking.

I know, some people say, "You can't do anything away from home that you couldn't do at home." I know the cost of a second room is ridiculously high, because everything is priced according to double occupancy standards. I know you are grown, single, divorced, or widowed, with kids and a full-time job and you pay all your own bills. I know you believe you can handle yourself in almost any situation. And I also know this is different. I know what it's like to get caught up in the pleasure and pageantry of a vacation getaway from all that responsibility. I know life is full of tough choices, and I know the decision to travel with a man (should you choose to do so) can deliver a major blow to your plan for living a *Single, Saved & Celibate* lifestyle, if you are not very careful.

Accountability Key: When it comes to travel, *accountability* is like super glue—a little goes a long way. It is not necessary to share your plans with everyone. Pick one or two people you trust, and make yourself accountable to them. The people you choose do not have to be Super Saints. They just need to be fellow believers (preferably female) who have agreed to live life according to a shared standard of *accountability*. If you cannot find one or two singles to covenant with, you might want to consider what that says about your circle of friends. If no one you are close to can be trusted to support your decision to live *Saved and Celibate,* that's a wake-up call. It may be time to consider extending your friendship network. And while you are at it, stop and consider which of your friends would say she can count on you as an *accountability* partner.

If you find you don't presently have any single friends who qualify, you can choose a married saint to touch and agree with; however, I have found the single/married type of *accountability* match can lead to a subtle inequality in relationship. If both are not deliberately working on balance, the married individual may misinterpret her role and set herself up as the "moral police officer." Conversations about travel and mutual *accountability* may erode into interrogation sessions. *Accountability* does not mean policing. *Accountability* in this context is a voluntary practice. If forced upon another individual, *accountability* ends up being punishment; something used to condemn and diminish, rather than encourage and uplift.

So my admonition to *Real Women* seeking *accountability* support is to choose wisely. And after having chosen, to be faithful to the process. It is never easy to admit our frailties and our faults to another human being, but God wants us to do in anyway *(James 5:16)*. Not so that we can sit in judgment of one another, but rather so that we can help one another get up and keep striving to be all that God wants us to be *(Galatians 6:1-4; Romans 15: 1-2)*.

One of the reasons *accountability* is such a powerful tool is because just knowing it is in place increases the likelihood that we will stop and think about our intentions before we take action. *Accountability* has a way of bringing what we do in the dark into the light. Remembering you are committed to share your struggles, successes, and failures with your *accountability* partner will likely help you make different choices, both in public and behind closed doors.

One additional note about *accountability*: Be prepared to resent it. Whether it be because your *accountability* partner's approach lacks finesse, or because you just don't feel like telling anyone your personal business on that particular day, *accountability* will not always feel good. Handle the discomfort by recognizing what is going on with you and taking some time to pray about how you will response to the feelings evoked. Above all else, try to remember that your *accountability* partner is there to help and not harm you. It also may help to remember that you asked your partner to be faithful, even when it was difficult to confront you. Finally, thank God for this person's ministry into your life. Someone caring enough about you to actually hold you accountable is a blessing, and the relationship should never be taken for granted.

LESSON #7

Being Enslaved by Liberation

The simple truth is most *Real Women* miss having sex—at least every now and then—otherwise, there would not be a need to learn how to practice celibacy. It seems fairly obvious; it's the things I enjoy that my flesh desires, and sexual contact is one of those things. Sex feels good, and it serves to meet a need in most of our lives. Otherwise, it wouldn't be so easy for the enemy to use sex to tempt us to step out of God's will. Yet, somehow we've been led to believe that celibacy requires that we learn to dislike the very act of sex. Some *Real Women* have even been taught that sex is inherently bad or harmful. In fact, these women internalize the message so well, they begin denying their true feelings. Ironically, the more we publicly deny our penchant for sexual pleasure, the more we privately crave it. And the more we crave sexual contact, the more likely we are to act out. And the more we act out, the more guilty and convicted we feel. And the more guilty and convicted we feel, the more the enemy tells us that we will never manage to live a celibate life.

It is a vicious cycle. Many of us go around and around, stuck on the wheel, until we simply give up and settle for living saved as a friend of mine says, "From the waist up." I'm here to tell you, that particular spirit

49

of hopelessness is a lie from the pit of hell. You *can* live *Single, Saved and Celibate*—and be satisfied doing it. What most of us can not do, however, is get there by denying that we were designed to enjoy sex.

Denying the physical pleasure of sex is only part of the reason we have such a difficult time maintaining our celibacy. Even while we are busy denying our desire for sex, we are bombarded with written, visual, verbal, and nonverbal sexual messages that scream for our attention. When we are more consciously aware of our own desires, we are more capable of sorting through and filtering these messages.

Conversely, when we are wrapped up in believing and convincing ourselves and others that we simply no longer struggle with our sexuality, we leave ourselves vulnerable to attack. Think about it; isn't saying to myself "I don't really like or want a slice of chocolate cake" actually more likely to lead me to secretly obsess over it? As I passed the cake plate during the day, I may force my eyes to look away, but in my heart, I'm remembering what it tasted like. Others may admire my resolve and even tell me how much they wish they would "be like me" and "just not crave sweets." This kind of feedback will, of course, serve to reinforce my denial. Now that others have acknowledged (and perhaps envied) my resolve and maturity, I don't dare tell anyone that the image of chocolate cake has now managed to find its way into my nearly every waking thought. Finally, when no one is looking, late in the night perhaps, I slip out of bed and hurriedly devour a small slice of the satisfaction I crave. I may replace the cover and wash my dish so that no one else will suspect, but inside I feel weak and ashamed. These feelings, however, may not stop me from continuing to sneak small pieces of pleasure until eventually (when caught) I simply declare myself to be "weak" or "grown" and accept the fact that chocolate cake is in my life to stay. Sound familiar?

We are all, at least in part, products our own environment. Many of us grew up in the 1960s, 1970s, or 1980s, when society's messages about sex were in direct conflict with what we were learning in Sunday school and church, just as is true today.

The 1960s was a decade of "free love." Smoking pot was the national pastime, and physical pleasure outside of the sanctity of marriage was not only permissible but was often promoted as the preferred lifestyle. We all knew people, or even were people, who were living together, paying bills, and raising children without the benefit of marriage. Toward the end of the decade, we even afforded these unions legitimacy by referring to them as "common-law" marriages, in an effort to eliminate any stigma and elevate relations outside of marriage to an equal status with marriage.

Then along came the 1970s. Our motto became "love the one you're with." It was the era of love songs, Afropuffs, *Soul Train,* cutoff shorts, midriff tops, and micro-mini dresses (sizzlers.) But unlike the era that ushered in the barefoot, tattooed, pot-smoking, laid-back generation of the 1960s, the 1970s were ruled by economics. We had money to spend, and we spent it on things that showed off how very sexy we were. The power of sex was also portrayed in the media. *Real Women* were large and in charge of their sexuality, and began starring in films and on TV. They alone chose who came in and out of their beds. We saw them using men and casting them aside, a kind of role reversal that excited us and gave us the illusion of power. We were being taught it was okay to use sex to get what we wanted, and the fact that it worked caused us to believe it was better than okay, it was justice.

The 1980s ushered in a wave of greed and selfish ambition the likes of which we as *Real Women* had never experienced. We didn't want anybody to give us anything, as James Brown said earlier, "Just open up the door and I'll get it myself." We learned to fight like a man in the boardroom, and we kept right on fighting once we got to the bedroom. We were told we did not need a man to tell us what to do, and that children would ruin our life and derail our career aspirations. We responded by taking responsibility for ourselves. Birth-control pills, diaphragms, and IUDs flew off the shelves, and again we used sex to fill in the gaps of our lives whenever we needed reassurance, external validation, or simply a physical release.

The 1990s caught us like deer in the proverbial headlights, stunned and amazed at the impact of the AIDS epidemic on our communities. Then, after catching our collective breath, we simply dismissed the whole thing as a white gay male or intravenous drug user's problem. We went right on having sex with men we were not married to. Only now, we took the time to ask if they had ever been on drugs or ever had gay sex. As if those were the only ways they could contract AIDS, and as if the men we were "dating" would dare tell us the truth before sleeping with us anyway, just because we asked.

All of this sexually liberating behavior has been going on, mind you, while we have been sitting in church Sunday after Sunday, pretending sex is not an issue for us. Is it any wonder we lack the power and the tools to achieve and maintain celibacy? The world is masterful at teaching us how to do sex their way. There are TV shows, movies, books, DVDs, CDs, all manner of sources to explain not just what you should do (whatever feels good) but *how* you can do it. In the world, being blatant and upfront about your sex life is applauded and encouraged. And if you need help discovering how to be a better lover, or how to attract a man sexually, help is readily available.

Conversely, in the Christian community, we simply tell people, "Don't have sex until you are married." Recently, we have added a sub-text describing why sex outside of marriage is bad for you. But we have managed to leave a huge void in the place where *how* to remain celibate belongs. As a whole, Christian singles understand the mandate to abstain from premarital sex, but precious few have been given the necessary tools to help them do so.

This book is designed to teach you a few of the "how-to's." It is intended to give you practical tools to manage your sexuality and your relationships in a way that works for you and honors God. This chapter is designed to help you explore your thoughts and feelings about sex. Learning how to view sex from a healthy Christ-centered perspective is important. God designed sex not just for procreation, but also for your enjoyment. We can get so mixed up in sin that we confuse the healthy sexual feelings we are having and label the feelings instead of the behavior as "wrong." Feeling good about sex is something that God understands and intended for us to experience. Think of it this way—if the act of sex were a high-performance automobile, you could drive that automobile on a dirt road or on an asphalt highway and it would feel okay, maybe even really good, especially at high speeds. But the feeling doesn't come anywhere close to the way it feels to drive the same high-performance automobile full out on the Autobahn in Germany. That stretch of road was specially designed and constructed for the activity, and the feeling of driving there has been compared to the sensation of flying. Of course, it is hard to know the difference if you've never experienced the latter, but it does make sense once you stop and take the time to think about it. God designed sex to be enjoyed inside of a committed marriage relationship. Logically, a marriage relationship is the ideal environment for optimal performance and sexual enjoyment.

In fact, if we can stop just doing whatever feels good at the moment and think about what we really want in a sexual relationship, we would have to admit that we want it all. *Real Women* really want the ultimate experience—excitement, pleasure, and mutual enjoyment, without guilt or remorse. We want God's blessing on our union. And the only way to get it all is to align our sex life with God's plan. God cannot contradict Himself. He will not bless any behavior that is contrary to His Word. That does not mean He won't bless you. He may even continue to bless your relationship, generally speaking; however, the future health and happiness of the sexual aspects of your relationship will be affected (positively or negatively) by whether or not your sex life flows in or out of God's design.

If you are a person who has never really enjoyed the physical act of sex, but who has been sexually active nonetheless, it is time to do some work on this area. Sometimes, for example due to trauma from abuse, we can teach ourselves to disassociate during sex. This means while our body is present during the act of sex, our mind and conscious awareness of what is happening is somewhere else. What served as a protective barrier for us earlier in life can be a detriment to us when attempting to build healthy sexual relationship with our mate.

Even without early trauma, some of us simply learn to use the physical act of sex as collateral to get to what we want (i.e. security, money, validation) from a man. In those scenarios, the act of sex is not as important as what it earns us. Years of this kind of behavior can produce a similar dissociative effect, in that we teach ourselves to become sexual manipulators, and in doing so, we make sex a job, rather than a privilege. Eventually, sex becomes "no big deal," and we convince ourselves that celibacy is at best overrated, and at worst unnecessary. In so doing, we become slaves to our own sexual liberation. Talk about a trap! The enemy is indeed crafty, but our God is both all-knowing (omniscient) and all-powerful (omnipotent). He understands the trap and will provide a way to get out of it *(I Corinthians 10:13)*. You are not reading this book or this chapter by accident. There are no coincidences in God's plan or design.

If your view or perception of sex has been clouded or tainted by either the world's messages or your own actions, now is the time to acknowledge the truth and decide whether you are ready to heal.

Once healing begins, many *Real Women* struggle with the quandary of how to retain the essence of their sensuality while attempting to remain celibate. Most *Real Women* are not virgins and they are not naïve innocents. *Real Women* tend to enjoy their femininity. We like being women, we like being noticed, we rather enjoy being complimented, and we have been known to flirt (appropriately, of course) when an attractive man crosses our path. If the cost of *Getting It All* amounts to us becoming cold, unattractive, asexual beings, the price is simply too high to pay. I do not believe God intended for us to stop being the vibrant, attractive, sensual women He created us to be. On the contrary, rather than abandoning our sensuality, we are required to protect and cherish the special gifts God has given us as *Real Women*. I view our sensuality as the essence of our womanhood. I believe it was Eve's sensuality that Adam first responded to when he awoke and discovered God had created a helpmate suitable for him. *(Genesis 2:18, 23.)* And I believe it is our responsibility to make wise decisions about when and with whom we share how God has so masterfully created us. We are far too rare, far too precious to be on display or to be available to just any man who happens by. We are unique and wonderfully made. Each of us is a one-of-a-kind masterpiece, handcrafted by the Creator of heaven and Earth. Never let anyone convince you to underestimate your value. Resist the urge to trade your God-given sensuality for the emptiness of conventional sexuality. Ultimately, the decision is yours.

If you are ready to trust your body as well as your spirit to the Lord Jesus Christ; If you are truly tired of being saved "from the waist up," pray this prayer now and every time you feel tempted to give up on your decision to live *Single, Saved & Celibate:*

Lord Jesus,

I commit my mind <u>and</u> my body to you today. I confess that I am tempted to give up my celibacy right now. But deep in my heart I know you created me for something better and you want me to have it all. Help me to get past this moment. Your Word says you will not give me more than I can bear; and if it gets too tough, you will provide a way of escape. Please help me to see that way and help me to take that way up and out of this situation. I trust you and you alone with my life; and that includes my sex life.

Amen.

LESSON #8

Lost in Love

Being in love feels good. How much more so for a *Real Woman* who has been previously unlucky in love? You have fought, struggled, fussed, and cussed your way into, through, and out of casual dating hell, and at last, you belong to the man you've been waiting for. He calls and text messages you throughout the day just to say hello. He makes you laugh, and you still catch yourself daydreaming about special moments. He's hinting about a future together, as men are prone to do, and you are lingering just a bit longer over bridal magazines—when no one is looking, of course. You are officially in love, and trust me, everybody knows it.

So what's the problem? Perhaps nothing at all. You may be the rare individual who can absorb all of the wonderful new experiences and sensations a relationship brings into your life without losing balance and perspective. Or you could be like most of us who lack practice being part of a healthy romantic relationship, and find yourself literally *lost in love*. How can you tell the difference?

We can all easily identify the black-and-white hallmarks of being *lost in love*. We have all known women who totally remake themselves to obtain or keep a man, as well as those who stubbornly pronounce their refusal to change any portion of their lives to satisfy anyone, especially a man. The extremes are just that, extreme; and it certainly doesn't take any sort of sophisticated behavioral analysis to see how damaging the extreme behavioral choices can be. It is the bothersome gray-area behaviors (I call them behavioral detours) that are so much more difficult to tease out. The following is a description of a few common behavioral detours. If you recognize any of these behaviors in yourself, note that your actions may be an indicator that you have strayed off the healthy relationship path and are in danger of becoming *lost in love*. The good news is, the sooner you recognize the detour, the sooner you can redirect your emotional compass, course correct your behavior, and get yourself back on track. Remember, the more important this relationship is to you, the more important it is for you to keep your part of the partnership (meaning you) healthy and on course.

Behavioral Detour #1: Hypersensitivity or "What does that mean?"

Some *Real Women* have become so accustomed to things going wrong in a romantic relationship that we are constantly waiting for the other shoe to drop. We live life on the emotional edge, over-interpreting every facial expression or vocal intonation as an indicator that he has changed the way he feels. We ask "What's wrong?" several times a day, and are never quite satisfied with the answer, "Nothing." If our man doesn't notice us enter a room anymore, or if he refuses to turn off the game to cuddle, we begin worrying that he may be bored and looking for someone else. We pout and whine or just plain get angry when in actuality, he really has not said or done anything wrong.

The problem is, we have gone from just appreciating the attention and adoration that is a natural part of a new relationship to actually needing constant attention and adoration in order to feel good about ourselves. Our past and our insecurities can lead us to search for deeper meaning in almost everything. We mislabel the normal leveling-off process that happens in all relationships as possible rejection. Because human beings have a tendency to interpret others' actions through their own behavioral lens, we surmise that the lack of intense contact and attention must spell doom. Fear mixes with anger, and we begin to alternate between crying, "Don't you love me anymore?" and yelling, "I don't have to put up with this!" In the process, we morph into someone who doesn't even remotely resemble the woman he fell in love with. The real you is now *lost in love.* And once lost, old survival instincts have a way of kicking in. Our distorted view of history reminds us that when all else fails, sex is a way to hang on to the relationship. The memory is distorted because the truth is, if sex was all it took to maintain a relationship, you would still be with the last man you were sleeping with. Don't be fooled and don't fool yourself into making the trade. In the long run, it just won't work.

Behavioral Detour #2: Over-identification or "Your life is my life."

Remember when you not only had an opinion about most things (art, politics, sports, current events, wardrobe, etc.) but you would actually state your opinion? Further, you and your partner enjoyed the lively debate differences in perspective could spark. Remember when you laughed about how different your tastes ran? You were two distinct individuals who agreed to try each other's preferences, but who maintained your own individual style, flair, opinions, and interests.

Is that still the case? Or have you traded in your opinions and interests for his? Have you given up personal hobbies and activities that use to be an important part of a balanced and healthy lifestyle? Did you use to work out to help manage stress, but just can't make time to get to the gym now that you have a man? Did you use to get together with your friends to hang out once or twice a month, but just don't have time to keep in touch anymore? Worse still, have you become one of those women who can't spend an evening with her friends free of continuous cell phone or text messaging contacts with her man? Do you find yourself squeezing your family and friends into whatever space is left open, only because your man has something else he needs to do without you? Do you catch yourself "checking in" when you are supposed to be enjoying someone else's company? Do you put your family and friends on a time clock, finishing your time with them as quickly as possible "just in case" your man shows up and wants to do something?

The real danger of being emotionally tethered to another human being this way is that you begin to feel less like his partner and more like his possession. And once you fall into that cycle, it can be a very slippery slope from there to a sexual relationship. The reason is because the more you give away the power to choose what you will and will not think, do, or tolerate, the easier it becomes to allow someone else to decide if you should or should not have sex. Before you know it, your sexual identity is defined by being some man's woman, instead of being God's child. Once that happens, all the rules change and you are left vulnerable to respond based on the shaky foundation of feelings, rather than the secure foundation of His Word.

I have learned that the old saying, "If both of us are always thinking the same thing, doing the same thing, saying the same thing, one of us is unnecessary" is absolutely true. You are a unique and special being, with your own thoughts, ideas, and opinions. Be careful not to sacrifice the unique and special part of who you are for this or any relationship.

A word of caution is warranted here. Please do not confuse the need for self-expression with the impulse to refuse compromise. The act of meeting in the middle is an important element of any healthy relationship. "My way or the highway" is an antiquated and lonely notion. I am not suggesting you refuse to give a little in terms of your time and interests. What I am talking about here is resisting the urge to simply become a subset of your man's life, because such behavior can lead to enmeshment and unhealthy over-identification with your partner.

Prior to marriage, and to a certain (much lesser) extent even after marriage, healthy couples maintain their own individual interests as well as joining together to experience shared or mutual interests.

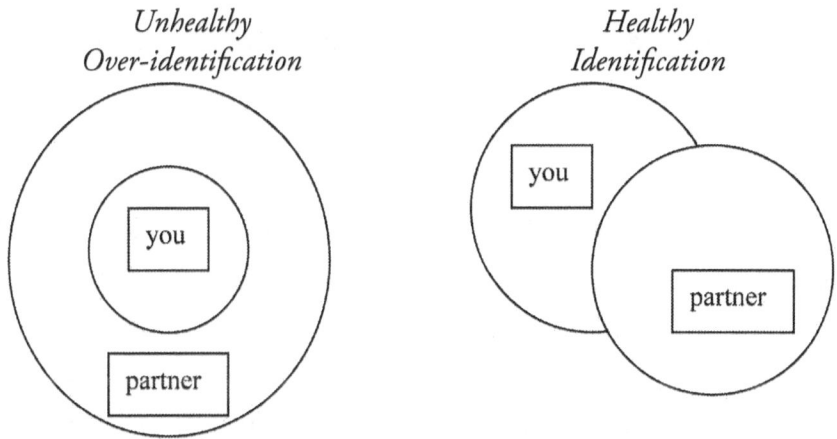

Behavioral Detour #3: Attention Suffocation or "Killing him with kindness."

Closely related to hypersensitivity, attention suffocation happens when a woman feels she can never do too much for her man. She may cook and clean for him as though she were his wife. If he's without transportation, she might find a ride or take public transit while he drives her car. She might buy him expensive gifts, help pay his bills (to the detriment of her own), and care for his children from previous relationships, all in an effort to express her love. In sum, fulfilling his needs, alleviating his stress, lightening his load, is her primary concern. Whether or not he reciprocates in like fashion really isn't the issue, but for the record, I've found it rarely to be the case that he does.

The real problem with this scenario is that the roles are reversed. God sets the order of a healthy relationship as the man working to care for, provide for, and protect the woman, the way Christ does for the church *(Ephesians 5:25)*. This is the essence of what it means to become a man. If you reduce a man to the status of a helpless child by providing for his every need, you become less like his woman and more like his mother. And what happens when a mother spoils her child to the point of overindulgence? Do her actions end up helping or hurting him in the long run?

Again, the feeling of being desperately needed is *satisfying*. The action of responding to meet that desperate need is *codependency*. The sense of empowerment that comes along with the ability to control another's mood or behavior with your response is *dangerous*. Power can be heady stuff. Being needed and responding in an unhealthy manner over time can result in a normalizing effect. After a while, you taking care of your man's every need may just feel normal. So much so that you may in fact become a bit judgmental or critical of other women who don't "take care of their man" as well. When others raise concerns about you "acting like his wife," you may dismiss those concerns as jealousy. At the end of the day, it might seem like the most natural thing in the world for him to require that you also meet his sexual needs. After all, the bedroom is the one place where he can still feel like a grown man, right? How could you deny him that one thing when you know what he's going through, how much stress he's under, etc. Sound familiar? Being *lost in love* can kind of sneak up on you. No self-respecting *Real Woman* sets out to lose her identity and become totally enmeshed with a man, but it happens. Take a moment and honestly evaluate whether you are presently *lost in love*.

LESSON #9

Facing Our Failures

Allow me to say once again, for the record, *none of us is perfect.* We have all sinned and fallen short of God's glory *(Romans 3:23)*. And that failure may include falling to sexual temptation.

I am no stranger to failure. While I am a veritable *Superwoman* in every other significant area of my life (work, ministry, parenting, community service, etc.), I struggled for years with one failed relationship after another. I was married and divorced twice before my thirtieth birthday. My third marriage ended in the sudden and unexpected death of the man I considered my soul mate. I spent many years angry, frustrated, lonely, and confused. I lost count of how many men I dated, and it still hurts to recall how many I had sex with. The one thing I'm certain of is that I didn't really love any of them. And in retrospect, they clearly didn't love me, at lest not as scripture defines love. I was using them and they were using me. We exchanged pain (disguised as pleasure) while desperately hoping God would bless the mess we had created. It all seems so crazy now, but back then, the enemy made me believe that was all there was left for me.

Through it all, I learned two very valuable lessons:

1. God loves, forgives and restores, and

2. Real Women sometimes fail.

Believe it or not, the second lesson was the harder one for me to acknowledge. *Real Women* are so use to succeeding in whatever we choose to do, that failure becomes our worst nightmare. We are embarrassed by it, and that embarrassment makes us vulnerable to compromise. We want so desperately to check off this one heretofore unachievable goal (namely being in a healthy, committed relationship) that we are willing to compromise our bodies and thus our relationship with the Lord to get it *(Galatians 3:8; 5:1)*.

Know that you are not alone in your struggle to change. Don't allow the enemy to convince you that it's too late, or that you've made too many mistakes to get it right now. Today is the day, now is the time. You're not so different. We've all been there. If a celibate lifestyle was easy to maintain, most of us would be enjoying a celibate lifestyle right now, and there would not be a need for this or any other book on the subject. If you've gotten this far (to Lesson #9) chances are pretty good you recognize that we all need tools to achieve and maintain our celibacy. One of those tools is honest self-evaluation of our failures.

One sure recipe for failure is the very human tendency to repeat the same unhealthy behavior over and over again, expecting a different result. Someone once said: That pattern is the very definition of insanity. I love the simplicity of the message espoused in the anonymous author's version of the following short story:

Life in Five Short Chapters

> *Chapter 1- I walk down the street. There's a hole in the sidewalk. I fall in. It takes a long time to get out.*

> *Chapter 2- I walk down the street. There's a hole in the sidewalk. I fall in. I can't believe I'm in the same place. I*

don't know why these things keep happening to me. It still takes a long time to get out.

Chapter 3 – I walk down the street. There's a hole in the sidewalk. My eyes are open, I see it, but I still fall in. It's a habit. I know where I am. It's my fault. I get out.

Chapter 4 – I walk down the street. I know there's a hole in the sidewalk. I walk around it.

Chapter 5 – I walk down another street.

When it comes to celibacy, many *Real Women* are stuck in *Chapter 1* or *Chapter 2,* walking down the same old relationship street. We have so much hidden shame and guilt around our relationship failures, it is painful to even bring the memories up. Instead, we pretend we have no idea how or why we keep ending up in the same dark place emotionally and physically. If we dare talk about our struggles at all, we are careful to do so in a way that implies our mistakes were part of our distant past. For some sick reason, we want everyone to think we have it all together. We want everyone to think we have figured this relationship thing completely out. We want everyone to think that struggles with our flesh are behind or beneath someone our age, with our spiritual maturity, given our level of responsibility, education, experience, etc.

The sad thing is, the more arrogant and dishonest we become, the more distance we put between our hurt and our healing. We lie so often about the power that sexual sin has over us that we sometimes begin to believe our own tales of victory. When we fail, we attempt to hide or cover it up by either harshly condemning those whose sexual failures are made public, or by simply disappearing from the very fellowship of believers we need to support our efforts to live holy.

No matter the choice, the basic inability to face our failures results in us being stuck in the same old dysfunctional behavior patterns.

Ladies, before another day passes, let's agree together that it's time to get out of the hole and learn how to walk down a different street. It can be as easy as steps one, two, and three. Let's begin by taking one step at a time together.

Step #1: "Opening Your Eyes"

There are two kinds of emotional or psychological "blinders." The first is when we ignore the data in front of us. The second is when we invent data (i.e. pretend things are said and done that were not). Opening your eyes and getting honest about what you see will allow you to deal effectively with both kinds of blindness.

Our resolve to achieve and maintain celibacy cannot succeed for long under blind and dishonest conditions. Living under those conditions is like trying to drive a car on a stormy night without windshield wipers. There is just too much stuff getting in the way. Seeing what is really there in your relationship is what chapters one through eight of this book are all about. Determine once and for all whether your relationship, as it stands, is conducive to living a celibate lifestyle. Are you struggling to maintain a relationship in which your partner is not committed to celibacy? Is yours an emotionally, physically, or spiritually abusive relationship? Are you traveling together, sharing a bed, and attempting to remain celibate? Have you so isolated yourself from family and close friends that this man has become your life? Are you choosing celibacy because it is the way you want to live your life or because you fear punishment or ridicule from God or man?

Conquering Step 1, *Opening Your Eyes,* involves making an honest assessment about your actions relative to relationships and sexuality.

Step 2: "Taking Responsibility"

Once you recognize and acknowledge the truth about where you are in terms of your relationship and your sexuality, your eyes are open. Welcome to life in *Chapter 3 (reference Life in Five Short Chapters, "Your Eyes Are Open")*

You are now prepared to *Take Responsibility*. You have walked down the same relationship street and fallen into the same hole. It's pretty much a habit at this point. The leading man may have changed over the years (or months), but you have basically been acting out the same story again and again and again. I think of it as sleepwalking through relationship hell. For too many years, I would wake up wondering how in the world I got myself right back into the same old mess (i.e. life in *Chapter 2*) Sound familiar? Well, take heart. This time, your eyes are open. You are fully aware of how you got here, and moreover, you are ready to take responsibility for your part in getting to this place.

In life, we make dozens of small decisions every day. In isolation, the weight of these decisions seems minimal, almost insignificant. But when you put all those small decisions together, you may begin to feel a very weighty pattern. Try viewing your life decisions from a slightly different perspective. Instead of thinking about what someone else *made* you do or what you *had* to do, try reframing your actions as things you *chose* to do. Instead of thinking "He made me mad," try thinking "I chose to get angry." Instead of wondering how you got to this place, try acknowledging the decisions you made that led you to this place.

Conquering Step 2 *(Taking Responsibility)* involves taking a totally honest look at *your part* in the relationship equation. Amazingly, that one small act will make it possible to move on to Step 3.

Step 3: "Walking Around the Hole"

Being in the neighborhood of sexual temptation and navigating around the trap is no easy feat. Yet there are times when the individual we are most likely to succumb to simply cannot be avoided altogether. If he works for the same company or attends the same church as you, each encounter can seem like an unfair test of sheer willpower. If we are not careful, we can convince ourselves that "friendship" and "politeness" warrant an occasional lunch or coffee, which may lead to dinner or a glass of wine at the end of a hard work week. And surprise, before you know it, you are faced with the danger of falling back into that same old familiar relationship hole, one in which your celibacy resolve will most certainly be tested.

But don't worry. You are wiser and stronger than you were in the past. Your eyes are open and you have taken responsibility for your own behavior. You have the power and the authority to walk around this challenge/hole. Pull on those cross-training shoes, ladies, and let's start walking!

The obvious strategies are the most effective. When at church, sit in front of rather than behind him, even if you have to move from your usual seat or pew to do so. If your church has more than one regularly scheduled worship service, choose the one he doesn't attend.

I know what you are thinking. Why should you have to change, move, be inconvenienced, etc.? Why can't *he* change? The answer is because life is not fair and because this isn't about him. This is about you taking care of you. If you are waiting for him to take care of you by moving to a different service or moving to a different church, yours will likely be a very long wait. It is never a good idea to give someone else that much control over your emotional well-being.

If you encounter him at work, it is best to employ a similar strategy. Having memorized his movements, you can anticipate what time he will be at the elevator, in the cafeteria, at the credit union, etc. So, you choose to be at those locations at a different time. Simply stated—stop running into him on accidental purpose. Instead, *Walk Around the Hole.*

Step 4: "Walking Down a Different Street"

Once you get used to walking around the hole, it becomes possible to *Walk Down a Different Street* altogether, emotionally if not literally. You do not have to waste energy focused on this person or his movements. You can move on with your life, in a healthy rather than a bitter way, such that you actually feel nothing negative or intense associated with this man being on the planet. You can make different choices, not just about how you handle individuals from past relationships, but also how you will handle sexual challenges in current and future relationships.

In this and previous chapters, we have already discussed four very common holes:

Hole #1: The Traveling hole
Hole #2: The Loneliness hole
Hole #3: The Abusive or Controlling Man hole
Hole #4: The I Have To See Him At Church and Work hole

In addition to these holes, years of helping *Real Women* overcome unhealthy behavior patterns has made me acutely aware of the following equally treacherous sinkholes:

Hole #5: The But He Looks So Good hole.

Trust me, a man who looks good enough to compel you to mess up over and over again knows it. More importantly, he will use the knowledge to get his way as often as possible. Ask yourself, when you became so shallow that a man's looks became more important than his character? Wake up Ladies! Snap out of it and see this man, see this relationship hole for what it is...a trap. Like your mama (or grandmamma) always said, "Beauty is only skin deep." Remember God is much more concerned about a man's heart than his looks. *(Luke 16:15; I Samuel 16:7)*

Hole #6: The But it Feels So Good hole

A first cousin to the *He Looks So Good* hole, the *It Feels So Good* hole reduces you to the sum of your physical parts. Your feelings have taken control of your thoughts. The more dependent you become on what *feels* good versus what *is* good for your life, the more likely it is you will be stuck in this hole. Chances are, when you get out of the hole, take responsibility for your choices, and see the trap for what it is, you may well find the strength to acknowledge that while the act itself *Feels So Good,* the treatment before and after (mixed with guilt and remorse), doesn't feel good at all. God's word is clear. A repeated pattern of sinful, self-indulgent behavior leads to destruction *(Ephesians 4:18-19)*.

Hole #7: The Sugar Daddy/Princess hole

Some *Real Women* have bought into the lie that the trappings of success are more important than happiness itself. We put up with disrespectful treatment and we compromise our values to be with men who can pay the price. We rationalize and justify our way into the same hole over and over, partially because the other women in our lives are envious of how well we are kept. We *like* the feeling of superiority others' feelings of jealousy give us.

The truth is, the money, the cars, the jewelry, the trips, the high-roller sexual liaisons, are *not* gifts; they are bribes. In exchange for money (or the things money can buy), we give our time, our talent, our bodies, and our peace of mind over to another individual. He takes and uses it (and us) at his leisure and at his pleasure. Not because he loves and respects us, but because he owns us, if only for a little while. Think about it, ladies. What he's offering isn't real treasure. In time it, will simply waste away *(Matthew 6:19-21)*.

Hole #8: The Better the Devil You Know hole

Fear and fatigue are the express elevators into the depths of this hole. Because we have invested significant time, money, and heartache into a relationship, we may simply decide to take the path of least resistance and settle for less than what God has for us. If we are not careful, the decision to compromise will lead to apathy. We can just get tired and decide to give up striving for anything better. This is the point where many *Real Women* buy into the lie that sexual compromise is a small price to pay to be in a committed relationship, while so many other women we know are spending their days and nights alone.

Remember, it is always a mistake to give up or give in to the negative message the enemy sends our way. Instead, keep pressing toward the mark *(Philippians 3:14)*. You are precious to the Savior who died for you *(I Peter 2:4-6)*. God wants to see you walk down a different street, and so do I.

LESSON #10

It's Not a Game; It's a Lifestyle

Celibacy is not a trick. It is not a way to finally get him to buy the ring, or get the really big house, or even to get him to stop seeing other people. Celibacy is a lifestyle. Having what my grandmother use to call "a made-up mind," and standing firm on the decision to maintain your celibacy is foundational to your spiritual and emotional health.

This is your life, not some lame soap opera or prime-time drama. Merely pretending to be committed to celibacy, while actually using your sexuality and the withholding of sex to manipulate others is a very dangerous game. God is neither pleased nor fooled by that kind of behavior. Even when you win, you lose *(Luke 17:33)*.

God wants us to rely on Him *(Matthew 6:33)*. When we compromise our spiritual dignity and self-worth to have a man in our life, what we are really saying is that we cannot rely on God to meet our emotional and physical needs. We are willing to trust Him with our work, our ministry, our children, and our finances, but we can't trust Him with the pain of our loneliness and our desire to be sexually active. If that's how you've seen things, I dare you to try trusting God with *everything* in your life, including your sexuality. I promise you, He's a great-big God, who can handle anything you can throw at Him. Besides, aren't you tired of carrying the load that routinely accompanies sexual sin?

For the *Real Women* who are just plain tired—tired of making the same mistakes over and over; tired of being separated from God; tired of not having any real power in their prayer or ministry life; tired of lying and covering up; tired of feeling guilty; tired of ending up right back where they started; the time for playing games is over. The time to call the question has arrived.

Are you a *Real Woman* who is ready to move that the person of Jesus Christ be Lord over your sexuality? If so, I'm certain the Holy Spirit will readily second the motion; and the blood shed on the cross will cover your past and open the door to a new future.

I am not going to lie to you or attempt to sugarcoat the truth. Achieving and maintaining celibacy is hard work. The good news is that you don't have to do it alone and you don't have to do it in your own strength. God wants to help you make better choices, just as you want to help your own children be the best they can be. God loves you, and He wants you to have it all. That is why He sent His Son to save you *(John 10:10)*.

Recommitting your physical body to Christ and choosing to practice a celibate lifestyle brings with it huge rewards. The first thing you gain when you stop sleeping with folk you are not married to is the opportunity to experience transformational change, which is change from the inside out. When practicing celibacy becomes a lifestyle, you get to experience what it's like to really be who God created you to be. As a consequence, you can grasp hold of God's true purpose for your life, and you will begin to realize that you can do anything. You will reach the logical conclusion that your happiness is not wrapped up in any man, except the person of Jesus Christ.

The second thing you gain from the decision to live a celibate lifestyle is freedom. You gain an incredible amount of freedom, chiefly because you have the ability to think clearly. The fog that has been blinding you and keeping you from making clear decisions about relationships evaporates. When you stop sleeping with folk you are not married to, you can better evaluate whether or not the relationship is beneficial to you. You can better determine whether the relationship is something you want to be part of. You can better determine whether this man deserves you, appreciates you, values you, or not.

The third thing you gain from the decision to live a celibate lifestyle is the ability to be honest. You no longer have to slink around anymore, pretending to be a Super Saint. You can be honest about your past, and once you get honest about your past, you can help someone else with their present. God wants you to use the stuff you have gone through to minister to other *Real Women*. Don't misunderstand; you took yourself to the dark, sad relationship place. God didn't put you there but He did allow you to be there, and more importantly, He brought you through it, so you could learn what you needed to learn. All of this so that ultimately you could use what you learned to give Him glory by ministering to someone else. When you keep the secret (including the lessons and the pain) to yourself, you block your blessing and someone else's.

The fourth thing you gain from the decision to live a celibate lifestyle is power. You gain power over sin and power over your own flesh. You develop greater self-discipline and a greater sense of self, resulting in the power to acknowledge that although you like sex, you are choosing to abstain. You gain the kind of power that will not allow the enemy to take your natural desires and distort them or use them against you. You gain power to stand against the pain, shame, and guilt that accompanies sin. You gain the power a single woman needs to manage her sexuality. You gain the power to understand what is going on with you.

Choosing celibacy as a lifestyle will give you the power to understand the value that God places on sex between a man and a woman. It will help you acknowledge that sex is something you enjoy, something you don't really want to have to give up, but something you are willing to cast aside so that you can be the woman that God wants you to be, until the time that He sets the environment where it is going to be right: within a committed marriage relationship. But it is important to remember that the Holy Spirit is a gentleman. He will prick you. He will remind you. He will knock. If you turn your back and refuse to listen to what the Lord is trying to reveal to you in the area of your sexuality; if you decide you do not want Him to interfere or access your sexuality, He will honor that decision and He will not force His way into your life. The Holy Spirit will just kind of allow you to wallow in the mess you have created. Eventually, even *Real Women* get sick and tired of being sick and tired, and we reach for help. But the damage that we do to ourselves (and to others) in the meantime is so unnecessary.

On the other hand, if you decide to trust Him and willingly allow Jesus to be Lord over your sexuality, He will give you what you need. If you want to trust Him and you are just not there yet, learn to pray:

"Lord, help me to do this, because I really don't know how."

The fifth thing you gain from the decision to live a celibate lifestyle is perhaps the most important. You gain a closer, more intimate relationship with the Lord. Trusting God with the most imitate part of yourself will never lead to disappointment. Think about it: He always returns your call. He always forgives you. He never brings up your past mistakes. He's always there to dry your tears. He's always willing to listen to your side. He always has your best interests at heart. He's always patient. He's always kind. He's never proud or boastful. He's never rude or self-seeking. He always rejoices in truth. He always protects you. He trusts you. He hopes for the best. His love has endured throughout your lifetime. In short, He is Love; Love that never, ever fails. *(I Corinthians 13:4-7)*.

Are you ready to experience the freedom, power, and intimacy that comes from a transformational lifestyle? If so, join me in making a commitment to live *Single, Saved & Celibate* today by repeating this prayer of commitment:

Lord Jesus,

I commit all that I am: my spirit, my mind, and my body to you today. I confess that I desire to be in a relationship and I am tempted to give up my celibacy right now in order to get (or keep) this man.

But deep in my heart, I know you created me for something better and you want me to have it all. Help me to get past this moment. Your Word says you will provide a way of escape. Please help me to see that way and help me to take that way up and out of this situation.

I trust you and you alone with my life, including my sex life. Please send me the man you have for me. In the meantime, help me to prepare my life and my heart and my body to receive what You have prepared for me.

I love You, Jesus, and I know and accept that You love me unconditionally. Thank you for understanding my pain and supplying my needs according to Your riches in Glory.

Amen.

Denise Lutcher Hadley, Psy.d.

Counseling Psychologist
Certified Alcohol & Drug Counselor
Senior Vice President, North
American Programs
Cityteam Ministries

Dr. Hadley is a graduate of Stanford University. She also holds a master's degree in educational psychology, with an emphasis in marriage, family, and child counseling and a doctorate of psychology from the University of San Francisco.

Over the past twenty-five years, Dr. Hadley has gained vast clinical experience working with various populations, including women in transition, couples, adolescents, children, HIV-positive clients, patients in residential treatment settings, juvenile offenders, and sexual abuse survivors. She also teaches at the undergraduate and graduate levels.

Dr. Hadley currently oversees the North American-based programs of CityTeam Ministries, a non-profit, non-denominational Christian community service agency serving the hungry and homeless in cities throughout the nation and through partnerships in several international locations.

In 1994, Dr. Hadley was commissioned to develop a residential treatment program for addicted, abused, and homeless women with children, with the goal of providing a vehicle for these women to become self-sufficient, contributing members of society. House of Grace remains one of the few programs where a woman can recover from her addiction without being forced to separate from her young children.

Dr. Hadley actively contributes to the community as a senior fellow of the American Leadership Forum-Silicon Valley, president of the National Coalition of 100 Black Women-Silicon Valley Chapter, as a member of Building Peaceful Families Board, and as a trustee at Maranatha Christian Center in San Jose, California. She is a 2005 recipient of the Dr. Martin Luther King, Jr. Association of Silicon Valley Good Neighbor Award, a 2004 recipient of the YWCA Tribute to Women and Industry Award, and a 2004 inductee into the Mt. Pleasant High School Hall of Fame.

Dr. Hadley is a native Californian. She currently makes her home in San Jose. She is the proud mother of three extraordinary children.

www.ingramcontent.com/pod-product-compliance
Lightning Source LLC
Chambersburg PA
CBHW031259280526
45784CB00004B/1912